T0198916

THE HONOR CYCLE

HOW TO GO FROM ENDURING FAMILY TO ENJOYING FAMILY

HARRISON WILDER

WestBow Press
PRESS
A DIVISION OF THOMAS NELSON

Unless otherwise noted, Scripture quotations are from the Holy Bible, New International Version®. NIV®. Copyright © 1973, 1978, 1984 by International Bible Society. Used by permission of Zondervan Publishing House.

WestBow Press books may be ordered through booksellers or by contacting:

WestBow Press
A Division of Thomas Nelson
1663 Liberty Drive
Bloomington, IN 47403
www.westbowpress.com
1-(866) 928-1240

ISBN: 978-1-4908-0354-8 (sc)
ISBN: 978-1-4908-0353-1 (hc)
ISBN: 978-1-4908-0355-5 (e)

Library of Congress Control Number: 2013913942

Printed in the United States of America.

WestBow Press rev. date: 11/19/2013

CONTENTS

INTRODUCTION

Our generation faces a significant dilemma. It's easy to be overwhelmed at the enormity of the global challenges we face—trillions in national debt, food and healthcare for billions of people, global warming, just to name a few. When faced with grave issues such as these, great generations throughout history arose courageously, tackling catastrophic challenges and building a better future for their children. We should do the same. Yet, our challenges are too big to face alone. Take our national debt. Even if we were to allocate ten percent of current federal revenue each year toward paying the debt down, it would take almost 70 years to pay it off. Without the commitment of our children toward a long-term solution, this problem will never be fixed. The same can be said for problems involving poverty and the environment.

We may set in motion great solutions for the future, but future generations must finish the work. Meanwhile, we need the experience of those older than us to help develop solutions. A prosperous future does not hinge just on you and me finding the courage to arise, but rather on many generations coming together, building one on the other.

I have realized that this holds true for my family as well. I've spent years trying to build a great future for my wife and young kids on my own. But I'm discovering that success for my family doesn't begin and end with my contribution. What's truly important is the ability to receive from my parents and others, build on it, and pass along what I've learned to my children. In the big picture, the relationship between generations becomes the key building block for the future. I think this is why the Bible constantly refers to God as the "God of Abraham, Isaac and Jacob." His plans for us are too big to be summed up in one generation. The full expression of God, His love and His plan for our lives is demonstrated across multiple generations as we advance together toward His promises.

The problem is that we're no longer equipped for generations to work together. We've lost touch with the fundamental practices that allow one to build on another. Our celebration of independence and individuality has inadvertently disrupted the cycle that allows us to build a legacy across multiple generations. As children, we feel responsible to achieve success on our own. As parents, we're so caught up pursuing our own dreams; we don't know how to invest in the next generation. As a result, family relationships are broken and we're not positioned to work together.

There is a natural cycle, however, that will create a thriving future from generation to generation. I call it the *Honor Cycle*. When properly cultivated, the Honor Cycle empowers families and societies to learn from their successes and failures, solve problems together and build a better future for those to come.

The Honor Cycle is initiated by two actions:

1) **Practicing Honor**
2) **Releasing Blessing**

An ancient Thai tradition illustrates how the Honor Cycle works. In the ceremony of Wai Khru, students pay homage to their teachers to express their gratitude and to formalize the student-teacher relationship. The student honors the teacher, recognizing the role of the teacher and submitting to his instruction. The *wai khru* chant, which expresses respect for the teachers, ends by asking that the teachers bless their studies.[1] This tradition demonstrates that the posture of the student is supremely important to facilitate the learning process. The student places value on the teacher and positions himself to receive what the teacher has to offer. But notice that the teacher understands that he must release blessing. Instruction and guidance is only part of the assignment. The real power of the older generation is to bless future generations!

A posture of honor positions us to receive blessing from our parents, teachers and mentors. Giving our blessing to our children, students and mentees empowers them to honor. This is the power of the Honor Cycle. Adhering to these simple principles can restore broken families and societies, setting them up to flourish for many generations.

Here are six insights to help you get the Honor Cycle working for you and your family

1) Honor Benefits You

Honor is not a cultural formality without relevance. On the contrary, it is hugely rewarding! You may know the 5th Commandment, "Honor your father and mother" (Ex. 20:12). Did you ever notice that it's the only one of the Ten Commandments that follows with a promise? "Honor your father and your mother...*that it may be well with you*" (Eph. 6:2-3). The practice of honor helps you make the most of your life. I list many of the benefits that I've seen in Chapter 2.

---

[1] Panrak, Patcharapol. "Sattahip navy school kids perform 'wai khru' ceremony." *Pattaya Mail.* Pattaya Mail Media Group, 1 July 2011. Web. 3 June 2013.

2) Honor is Probably Not What You Think It Is

Unfortunately, our society has lost touch with the true meaning and purpose of honor. "Honor" has become more about outward expressions of respect, rather than cultivating an internal sense of value for other people. The true meaning of honor is all about placing value on another person. I help you redefine what honor means in Chapter 3.

3) Honor Benefits Your Parents

You may not know it, but your parents and mentors have emotional needs just like you. One of their greatest needs is to know you value them. When you start practicing honor, they will become much more secure. In fact, you'll notice them becoming better in their role, which benefits you and keeps the Honor Cycle flowing! I show what honor does for your parents in Chapter 6.

4) Your Blessing Benefits Your Children

There is no greater power you have as a parent than to release blessing on your children. It shapes their sense of identity and purpose. Your words have the power to change your child's future, and your blessing is the key to help them receive everything you have to offer. It's an essential part of the Honor Cycle. I share the power of a simple blessing in Chapter 7.

5) You can Correct Negative Behavior and still Release a Blessing

As a father of young children, I recognize parenting is not about pretending your children are perfect. You have a responsibility to correct negative behavior. These moments, however, can be great opportunities to reinforce the Honor Cycle by taking time to speak a blessing while bringing correction. I talk about how to do this in Chapter 8.

6) **Releasing a Blessing is a Supernatural Process**

Are you ready to get spiritual? Faith in God will empower you to release blessing on a whole new level. Allowing God to be a part of the process will supercharge the power of the Honor Cycle and multiply your blessing for many generations to come. I show you how faith empowers you to bless in Chapter 9.

IS THE HONOR CYCLE ONLY FOR PARENTS AND CHILDREN?

As you read, don't allow yourself to get stuck on the words *parent* or *child*. The Honor Cycle works in all generational relationships. *Parent* could easily be replaced with *mentor, spiritual leader, boss* or *teacher*. *Child* could be substituted with *mentee, student, employee,* or *congregant*. I use examples throughout the book of these other relationships to illustrate how the Honor Cycle works.

PART ONE: PRACTICING HONOR

"The company of the prophets said to Elisha, 'Look, the place where we meet with you is too small for us. Let us go to the Jordan, where each of us can get a pole; and let us build a place there for us to meet.'

And he said, 'Go.'

Then one of them said, 'Won't you please come with your servants?'

'I will,' Elisha replied. And he went with them.

They went to the Jordan and began to cut down trees. As one of them was cutting down a tree, the iron axhead fell into the water. 'Oh no, my lord!' he cried out. 'It was borrowed!'

The man of God asked, 'Where did it fall?' When he showed him the place, Elisha cut a stick and threw it there, and made the iron float. 'Lift it out,' he said. Then the man reached out his hand and took it."

2 Kings 6:1-7

CHAPTER ONE

GETTING THE HONOR CYCLE MOVING

This story of Elisha and the axhead always seemed kind of random to me. I had probably read this story ten times before I finally stopped to question its meaning. Sandwiched between epic battles and miraculous healings is this little paragraph about an axe head floating in the water. What's the big deal? You can almost envision at least one scribe copying ancient manuscripts word for word a few thousand years ago, thinking he could save himself a hand cramp and just leave this part out.

The sons of the prophets came together to approach Elisha, their spiritual father. They had a plan. The place where they lived was too small for all of them. They believed they needed to expand into another area. So, they asked Elisha for his permission to start the expansion project. In a display of honor that would be rare today, they submitted their idea to a father. Elisha's response, in a display of trust that would also be rare today, was immediate support of the initiative. I'm sure Elisha's living quarters weren't cramped! He could have reminded them about how, when he grew up under his spiritual father Elijah, they walked everywhere (probably uphill both ways in three feet of snow and 100-degree weather). Instead, Elisha perceived the needs of a new generation to expand and permitted them to build a larger future for themselves.

The next sentence is what really gripped me. "Please! Come along with us!" This line in the story tugged at something in my heart. I realized that I couldn't relate to this request from the sons of the prophets. I would have been happy to leave Elisha and start building my future on my own. Somewhere deep inside, a part of me didn't want to bring the fathers in my life into my endeavors. A part of me wanted to escape their oversight and go it alone. I realized my independence stood in sharp contrast to the cries of the sons of the prophets, "Father, we don't want to go without you!"

They knew something that had eluded me—that they had no chance of building a better future for themselves unless they brought the previous generation along with them. Unlike me, they didn't see their father as a restriction on their future. In fact, they knew he brought a blessing to their work that they would not be able to provide on their own. In the end, they ran into a major setback, dropping the borrowed axhead into the water. And they didn't have a hardware store up the street! This mistake could have kept them from being able to move their plans forward for quite some time. Thankfully, Elisha, the father, had the solution to keep them moving forward[1].

This is the heart behind the Honor Cycle. There is a blessing that fathers and mothers have to offer the work of this generation. Moreover, there is a blessing that we have to offer future generations. We're uniquely positioned to build the future by not only focusing on our children but also by restoring the broken parts of relationships with parents. While we may choose to bless future generations, we *need* the blessing from previous generations to discover our own potential. I believe this is where the Honor Cycle starts: learning

---

1 Interpretation inspired by a message from Pastor Joe Champion at the 2011 Wave Leadership Summit.

how to open the door for blessing in our lives through the practice of honor, then discovering how to pass along that blessing to future generations.

Three Questions that Get the Honor Cycle Moving:

1) **How do you see your parents' generation?**
   Think about it for a minute. Do you see value in the previous generation? Given the chance to build something on your own, would you demand that they come and build with you? Or do you relish the opportunity to stand on your own without their oversight?

2) **How do you see the next generation?**
   Does your vision for the future go beyond your life? What are you invested in that will benefit future generations? Are you prepared to come alongside a new generation and empower them to flourish?

3) **Would you consider a new approach?**
   What if the Honor Cycle truly does have the power to transform our families and our society? Are you willing to change your lifestyle to take advantage of its power? The Honor Cycle won't self-initiate, but it only takes one willing person to get it moving in your family. Are you willing to consider a new approach to life and relationships?

CHAPTER TWO

THE COMMANDMENT WITH A PROMISE

This has been a long journey for me. I've spent the last fifteen years intentionally growing in the practice of honor. Of course, there are still days where I catch myself wanting to forge my own path. But I've seen the advantages of this lifestyle in ways I never could have expected. To be honest, I wasn't too excited about practicing honor at first. I was *willing*, because I had realized it was the right thing to do. When I started to grasp the potential benefits for me, then I became really motivated! Check out this reference to the Fifth Commandment in Ephesians:

> "'Honor your father and mother'—which is the first commandment with a promise—'so that it may go well with you and that you may enjoy long life on the earth'" (Eph. 6:2-3).

Here's where I get excited. Of all Ten Commandments, the commandment to honor your parents is the only one connected to a promise. And what a phenomenal promise! "So that it may go well with you and that you may enjoy long life on the earth." Honor doesn't simply flatter our parents; it is essential to our own success and livelihood!

For a long time, I thought of this promise as a purely spiritual challenge—that if I honored my parents when I was young, God would reward my achievement by miraculously extending my life and making me successful. While I believe there is an element of truth to that way of thinking, I now see a much more natural application. When we set out to honor our parents, *we* are actually the ones who benefit from the relationship. God wants us to engage in honoring relationships with our parents, because if we do, things will go well for *us*. Honoring our parents isn't some kind of spiritual merit badge. God is giving us valuable insight! When we honor, we benefit from our parents' lives, wisdom, failures and successes. We live longer and better simply because we can build on their foundation!

Here are five benefits of honoring relationships that I've seen over the years. Some are very practical. Some are very spiritual. I'm sure you could come up with your own list as you think about it.

Five Benefits of Practicing Honor

1) Honor brings the voice of experience
2) Honor helps us hear God and make better decisions
3) Honor brings covering
4) Honor brings stability
5) Honor sown is reaped in future generations

<u>Honor Brings the Voice of Experience</u>

Growing up, I often stood beside my father as he would tackle various home projects. My dad has probably rebuilt every piece of our 200-year-old family home in the decades that he's lived there.

On one occasion, my dad sent me to the tool shed to find something he needed. I darted across the yard, excited to be able to help, and stopped in the door-way of the tool shed. I started looking around for the tool he needed. I spent probably ten minutes frantically searching, feeling like a failure that I couldn't find the tool, worried that I would disappoint my dad. Finally it hit me. I had no idea what the tool that he had requested looked like!

For some reason, I spent most of my childhood thinking I was supposed to be able to do everything on my own. Years later, as I reflected back on my experience, remembering the frustration and disappointment I felt in myself, I realized that the perspective I had as a kid was completely skewed. I was just a child! I wasn't supposed to have all the answers! My father knew exactly what that mystery tool looked like. I needed only ask, and he would have been delighted to teach me what I needed to know to get the job done. By relying solely on my own knowhow, I spent most of my childhood neglecting one of my greatest assets: the life experience of my own parents. Rather than benefiting from what they could teach me, I got in the habit of trying to learn for myself what life had already taught them.

Insights from the Voice of Experience

The practice of honor positions you to benefit from the experiences of your parents and others. You assume a posture that learns from all they have to offer.

1) **Successes**

   Chances are your parents have done something right along the way. They made a good choice that paid off. They avoided some disaster that others fell into. Maybe they discovered a perspective on life that has kept them happy or made them prosperous. Honor will help you learn from their success.

2) **Failures**

Even if your parents have never made a single good choice, they still have a world of experience to offer you. Trust me, they know where they've screwed up. And I bet they don't want you to take the same path! Honor will help pull out of them the lessons they've learned from their failures.

3) **Knowledge**

Wouldn't it be a shame if every generation had to learn everything for itself? We would have to discover every invention and insight into our world all over again every generation. While that may seem ridiculous, it's often the approach we take toward our parents. Honor, however, will help us build on the foundation of knowledge they've already established.

4) **YOU**

That's right! Nobody has had more experience with you than your parents. Sometimes you need to step outside of yourself to understand why you are the way you are. Parents see things about you that you don't comprehend on your own. Honor will open up this well of experience and help you understand the greatest mystery of all... yourself!

I Have Something my Father Doesn't Have

My dad lost his father to a heart attack when my dad was just 18 years old. My father's childhood memories are the only guiding force of experience that his father was able to leave him. He didn't have his father to talk to him about how to be married or raise children, how to manage finances, or be a responsible citizen or successful businessman. He learned the value of that input because it wasn't always there for him. If you were my father, knowing the fragility of life, how would you go about raising your children? I expect you'd try to impart to them as much as you could from your own experience while you were still with them. Imagine how surprised you would be if your child didn't look to you for input but instead wanted to learn everything for himself. That can be hurtful for a parent, but really it's the child who misses out! I think about how happy my father still is to teach me everything he knows about that old house we grew up in. He's delighted to teach me all about the tools and the skills he's learned. But that's just the beginning. Honoring my father positions me to benefit from a whole life that started before me. I'm lucky my father is still with me through these years of my life. There are so many more important things in life than the name of a tool in a shed, and my father has so much to share with me about those things.

When I began to understand this principle of learning from my father's life experience, I soon found an opportunity to apply it. The week after I was reflecting on this experience with my father, I sat in our church office discussing a situation on the worship team with my Pastor. He was communicating a specific change he wanted that would improve the quality of our music and promote a greater level of excellence in the team. I was leading the worship team at the time, and I knew this change would be difficult. If I wasn't careful, I might even hurt the feelings of some of our team members. I knew our team could not continue to improve without making this important adjustment, but I worried that I didn't have the experience to handle communicating the change to the team.

I resolved to do my best and was about to walk out the door when I remembered what I had learned earlier that week. My Pastor had been a part of worship teams for many years of his ministry experience. Moreover, I figured that in leading our church he must have encountered many communication problems just like mine. I sat back down and asked him, "How would you handle this?" We talked through the issue in more detail and he laid out a communication strategy that saved me hours of agony and probably a lot of drama with our team members. His experience easily offered me a better path forward than I could have come up with on my own. And he was happy to provide it! This interchange honored his role as a father in my life and gave me insight into a better course of action.

Honor Helps us Hear God and Make Better Decisions

I used to think that hearing God about choices in life was like appearing before a judge for an up-down vote. The more spiritual you were, the more decisions God would weigh in on. "No, my child, don't wear the green tie. Wear the red one." "Ah-ah, not the black belt!" All kidding aside, while this kind of direction has its place, I've come to believe that God's preferred decision-making process involves us using what He's taught us. Instead of micromanaging from His throne, He wants us to make good decisions born out of a dialogue with Him, His Word, our experience and the input of mothers and fathers that He has already placed in our lives.

I'll never forget driving down Massachusetts Avenue in Southeast Washington, DC, having a one-way conversation with God about Eileen. Eileen is now my wife, but at the time, we had just discovered a mutual interest in each other. I was appearing before the judge (God) looking for an up-down vote on our relationship. I was asking what I thought were simple questions, "Is she THE ONE? Should we date each other? Can I take her to this musical?" I wasn't getting any response and began to get a bit frustrated, when suddenly God interrupted my stream of questions with a question of His own: "What do YOU think about her?" Honestly, the question caught me off guard. "What do you mean, 'what do I think'? Why does it matter what I think? You're the omnipotent God! I'm just supposed to take orders from You, right?!" But His question stuck with me and slowly began to change my perspective about how He wanted these conversations to go.

I'm sure many of you have been there. You're trying to make a big decision and the correct answer seems lost somewhere in a muddle of emotions, desires, and practical reasoning. You're paralyzed, hoping for God's booming voice of clarity to straighten things out, but it doesn't come. Why? The problem is that the up-down verdict is only one part of the entire decision-making process. God wants to be involved in all the other steps as well! When you begin to involve him in each step of the journey, you'll discover that God's way of decision-making comes with many growth opportunities.

Opportunities for Growth while Making Decisions

1) Explore Your Motives
2) Discover Alternative Options
3) Assess Your Strengths and Weaknesses
4) Confront Your Fears
5) Learn from Your past

My natural tendency is to speed through this process, skipping right to the up-down vote. But God is all about the journey, not merely the end result. He uses the process of decision making to shape our character. If you're going to learn to hear God better about your decisions, you must bring Him in to every part of the decision-making process.

The good news is that He's already put people in your life to help you along. They can ask the tough questions and challenge you with their wisdom and outside perspective. In fact, God placed your parents in your life for that very purpose. If you will honor them by inviting them into every level of your decision-making process, you will walk away from every decision with confidence that you're on the right track and that you've heard from God.

The Lord saith, "Get Married!"

A few years ago, a couple showed up for an appointment in my Pastor's office. They had been dating for a short time and had decided that God wanted them to marry. Both sets of their parents opposed them rushing into marriage. Meanwhile, the couple had come looking for my Pastor's blessing to move forward. It was clear they sought his quick stamp of approval, rather than his honest input on the relationship. And yet, they believed they had honored him by stopping by to receive his blessing. Had they given him a real choice? They were convinced they had heard God about their decision, and they postured themselves defensively, probably because no one else agreed with their hasty decision. Pastor could give them the thumbs up to avoid pushing them away from their church family, or he could question their decision and risk being thrown in the mud with the other naysayers. Some choice!

A true heart of honor will engage parents and other sources of authority long before arriving at a final decision. Driving down the road that night in Southeast DC, I saw that God wanted me to start a long process of discovery about Eileen and me. Over the next months of carefully building our relationship, we engaged our parents, our Pastors, and trusted friends in that process. Sometimes we didn't like what they had to say, but we honored it, prayed about it together, and over time we all came to the same consensus. By the time we stood on the altar a year later, we knew we had heard God about our marriage, and we have built our family on that solid foundation. The Bible says, "Those who trust in themselves are fools, but those who walk in wisdom are kept safe." (Prov. 28:26). When you try to hear the voice of God all on your own, you trust yourself to discern the difference between what He wants and what is your own mind, will and emotions. When you choose to practice honor, God uses others to sort through all of that and help you discover His voice amid the clutter.

Develop Honoring Relationships Before They're Needed
All of these benefits come out of an intentional relationship of honor. When you start with the relationship, the benefits are there when you

need them. It doesn't always work the other way around. I talk to many young men who face tough decisions. They want the voice of experience to guide them. They want help hearing God about their situations, but they feel awkward bringing it up with their parents. They don't even know how to begin the conversation. Most of the time, there is no honoring foundation in the relationship to work from. I've found that when you spend effort building that foundation, the benefits flow naturally. Don't wait until the need arises to start building these types of relationships. Examine your heart now. Set your heart to honor your parents. Engage them in your life and choices now, and the relationship will already be in place when you need it.

Honor Brings Covering

During my freshman year of college, I contemplated leaving DC and heading to Bible college in South Carolina. As usual, I tried to make the decision on my own without consulting anyone. I honestly didn't know what I should do. I knew I had a calling to ministry, and Bible school seemed like the best way to move forward, but I felt unsettled. I prayed and fasted while trying to decide, but couldn't find peace either way. Everything became foggy in my head. While praying one afternoon, I felt the Lord impress on my heart to talk to my Pastor and tell him that I wouldn't leave DC without his blessing. That night, while at the Pastor's house for a prayer meeting, I did exactly that.

What happened next surprised me. When I got in the car to drive away, I realized that I had a new clarity about the future. I was certain that God wanted me to stay in DC, and that I would be here for a long time. No more confusion, no lack of peace! I knew without a doubt that I was right where I was supposed to be. The interesting thing about this transformation was that my Pastor had said nothing to me! My seemingly random profession "I won't leave DC without your blessing" surely warranted no more than his awkward response. Yet that conversation had straightened everything out for me. I went to sleep that night anticipating the future with an unassailable peace. Only months later would I understand what had happened in that moment. By positioning myself to honor my Pastor, I had left a place of isolation and entered what I can only describe as a kind of covering. On my own, I lived in a world of confusion and uncertainty. A lone ranger with no bearings, I was often influenced by passing whims. Through this interchange with my Pastor, I had stumbled into one of the benefits of practicing honor—having a spiritual covering.

Psalm 91 teaches: "Whoever dwells in the shelter of the Most High will rest in the shadow of the Almighty. I will say of the Lord, 'He is my refuge and my fortress, my God, in whom I trust'" (Psalm 91:1-2). John Bevere uses this scripture as a springboard for discussing the concept of spiritual covering in his book, *Under Cover.*[1] Under God's covering, we're protected. But Bevere asserts that we're not truly under God's covering unless we're under the cover of His *delegated authority.* God has appointed certain people, like fathers, mothers, church leaders, and civil authorities, to cover us. When we run from those relationships, we run from God's covering. (See Romans 13:1.) When we honor those relationships, we come under His protection.

Benefits of Being Under Cover

1) Better Clarity for Decision-making (Prov. 3:6)
2) More Power over Temptation (James 4:7, Ps. 91:3)
3) Understanding and Empowerment for your Purpose (Eph. 1:18-22)
4) Greater Peace (2 Thess. 3:16, Phil. 4:6-7)
5) Healing (James 5:14-15)
6) Protection from Danger (Psalm 91)
7) Greater Insight in to God's Word (Mark 4:11)

---

[1] John Bevere, *Under Cover.* (Nashville: Thomas Nelson, Inc., 2001).

Under God's covering, you stand protected from natural and spiritual forces that you may not be prepared to face on your own. Like a parent who watches over the physical well being of a young child, God's delegated authority covers you spiritually.

I Couldn't Stop Kissing Her!

I've seen this principle of spiritual covering work countless times in my life and in the lives of others. One such occasion involved a relationship I had developed when I was still single. I had become close to a girl who was part of our church. We had been friends for over a year and had discussed briefly whether we should begin dating. We quickly realized we would be better off staying friends. The problem was, whenever we hung out, we always ended up making out. Afterward, we would agree not to see each other anymore. But within days we'd find ourselves right back in the same situation.

I was ashamed at my lack of self-control and hid the relationship from anyone who could help. After this went on for a while, we got frustrated enough to take action. I sat down with my Pastor and opened up about the whole thing. I was so embarrassed and felt like such a failure. It was so difficult for me to be vulnerable, but I didn't know what else to do, seeing the futility of my own efforts.

Immediately after I brought the matter to his attention, the whole cycle stopped. What I had been unable to shake on my own disappeared and was no longer even a temptation. I believe that the simple act of inviting a father into that situation brought a spiritual covering that helped me resist what I knew were poor choices, choices I had proved unable to resist on my own.

Thankful for the Covering

Sometimes I play out in my mind what my life would have been like if I had followed my own path and neglected to receive the input of my father and Pastor in those crucial years. The leadership of the Bible school I had planned to attend parted ways after an ugly dispute. Some friends of mine who attended during that time were so disillusioned by the experience that they walked away from God. Although some of them are doing great things for God, I don't know that they found true relationships with spiritual fathers and mothers like the ones that have carried me through the last decade. The benefits of those honoring relationships, both here and back in South Carolina, are also carrying me toward awesome things ahead.

Honor Brings Stability

My Pastor often describes the relationship of two generations as a river. The younger generation is like the water that is charging downstream, full of excitement, passion and fervor. The older generation is like the banks of the river that channel that water in the right direction. Imagine a river with no banks. The water would spread out all over the place, expending all of its energy in every direction until it was completely spent and worthless. Living life outside of honoring relationships with previous generations is a set-up for ineffectiveness and instability. The guidance of fathers and mothers focuses and channels youthful energy into a powerful force. Thus, when parents place limits on a child, they provide the stability necessary for the child's development.

Staying Planted and Putting Down Roots

A guy I knew growing up (I'll call him Steve) was always chomping at the bit to get away from home. When he was still a teenager, he decided that he was ready to start a new life in a different part of the country. However, his parents felt he was not prepared to face the world on his own. Steve rejected their input. Things went well at first, but after a year he began to experience the same urge to leave his environment. Again, his parents and mentors recommended he stay put. He decided they must not understand his needs, so he uprooted again and found a new community. This cycle repeated itself every few years of his young adult life. The reality is that Steve needed to undergo serious spiritual and emotional growth. There are some things you'll only learn by planting yourself in a stable community, facing difficult moments and growing through them. Every time things got too uncomfortable for Steve, he pulled up his roots and planted himself elsewhere.

Practicing honor can help you make the decision to stay planted in a stable environment that produces growth. When you may get restless and ready to try something new, parents can often see the areas where you may still need growth. They're hesitant to let you move on until you mature through those things. It can feel restricting, but it's just channeling your energy to face the things that really matter. Truth be told, when a child has matured in areas they were once weak, parents are generally the *first* people who want the child to leave the nest and test their wings. Honoring may mean yielding to parents' hesitations, knowing that they likely see areas where you need to grow before moving on.

Gifts vs. Fruits

Fleeing uncomfortable situations is not the only reason you might want to uproot from an otherwise stable environment. Sometimes you'll be driven by an opportunity to chase a dream or to use your unique, God-given talents in some special way. Chasing opportunities like these is thrilling, especially when they have the potential to make a real difference in the world. However, pursued at the wrong time, these pursuits can actually stunt your growth. It's like the proverbial kid who wants to join the circus. Who wouldn't like to travel around, see the world, amaze others with your talents, and hear the roar of the crowd every day of the week? We find value in ourselves when people appreciate our skills and talents, i.e. when we're doing what we were created to do! Parents, however, see things from a unique perspective. Beyond the development of your *gifts*, they see the *fruit* your life is producing.

Gifts are easy to come by. Everyone has them. They certainly require some work to develop, but initially they're free. They don't cost us anything, and they don't require maturity to use them. Fruit, on the other hand, comes only when we let our roots reach deep into good soil. Fruit is the result of a maturing process in a stable environment. It comes by engaging in relationships and facing circumstances head on, not running away from them. Mature parents tend to focus on fruits, not gifts. Why? Because of experience! They know that in the end, the fruit of your life is what determines whether you succeed or fail, and whether you have a lonely and miserable life, or one full of exuberance and real friendships. They know that wherever your gifts take you in life, it is the fruits of maturity that ultimately will sustain you.

Fruits are things like love, joy, peace, longsuffering, kindness, goodness, faithfulness, meekness, and self-control. (Galatians 5:22-23) Their development requires patience, honesty, loyalty, hope and the ability to trust. We don't produce these fruits when we're jealous, bitter, proud, selfish or quick-tempered. (1 Cor. 13:4-7) These virtues will determine our long-term success, and we should value and pursue them with even greater zeal than we pursue gifts and talents. The Bible challenges us to eagerly desire gifts (1 Cor. 12:31), but also teaches that we will be judged not by gifts, but by our fruit! (Matt. 7:16-23) The use of our gifts, if not accompanied by good fruit, will ultimately amount to nothing. (1 Cor. 13:1-3) Parents will help keep your focus in the right place so that you don't spend all your time chasing gifts, thereby missing opportunities to develop fruit. .

Planted things Flourish

My Pastor has always taught me the value of being "planted." If a plant is continually moved, it will never grow, because it won't have a chance to spread out and develop deep roots. The same is true for people. Only when we resolve to really engage and connect with our community, will we see real growth and the reward of producing great fruit. "The righteous will flourish like a palm tree...*planted* in the house of the Lord, they will flourish in the courts of our God. They will still bear fruit in old age, they will stay fresh and green" (Psalm 92:13, emphasis added). This is not to say you should never move! You may need to transplant yourself from time to time, but when you do, it should be because you've matured and are ready to tackle new areas of development in the next location. Parents are great sources of input to see if you're ready to move on, still need some maturing, or perhaps could better mature in a different environment.

During a recent trip to Brazil, I ran into a young friend of mine. The last time I had seen him, he was finishing up high school in his home state of North Carolina. At that time, he was full of vision and excitement for his future. When I saw him in Brazil, I mentioned my surprise at seeing him on his own, given that he had just graduated high school the year before. I asked how he had wound up there. He told me that though he had grown up in a small town, the vision God had put in his heart is big. His parents decided that spending nine months to a year with the church in Brazil would be a great way to help him develop that vision. His growth was evident. He had matured significantly in a short amount of time. His story confirmed to me that parents not only promote stability in our development, but also know when it's important to make sure we're exposed to the right environment for continued growth. I'm so proud of this young man who is experiencing the benefits of an honoring relationship with his parents. I know he will undoubtedly realize the great vision in his heart.

Honor Sown is Reaped in Future Generations

The Bible says, "A man reaps what he sows" (Galatians 6:7b). I've been able to apply this concept to many areas of life—forgiveness, generosity, friendliness, as well as my thoughts, words, and actions. It also works across generations. Hopefully you haven't heard this personally, but sometimes a frustrated parent will blurt the phrase: "One day you're going to have a kid just like you!" They're basically telling the child that he's going to reap what he has sown. This principle is true, so sometimes the parent ends up being right! To those of you sowing dishonor and rebellion, look out! No matter what good things you may have sown in other areas of life, those seeds of dishonor will work against you. If you reject what your parents have to offer you, your children may reject your successes and the lessons you've learned. This robs your ability to pass good things along to future generations, destroying any opportunity of your family to grow stronger over time.

The One-Term Great Awakening

At certain times throughout history, whole people groups have experienced an intensifying of their faith in God and have been motivated to draw closer to Him. I've often wondered why these "awakenings" are so short-lived and don't seem to pass easily from generation to generation. I suspect one reason is because it's easy for seeds of dishonor to be mixed in with spiritual awakening. A generation who experiences God in a new way can easily develop a spiritual pride that causes them to judge and condemn previous generations who experienced God a different way. Even though the new generation is encountering God and sowing great seeds of righteousness, the seeds of dishonor are also bearing fruit in the next generation. If a generation does not sow honor into their parents' generation, they will fail to reap honor from the generations that follow. Even if we experienced a great awakening in our generation, if we dishonored our parents' experience of faith, the next generation would likely rebel against what we have to teach them. The dishonor we sowed would be reaped in our children and bring our "awakening" to a screeching halt.

Are we doomed to fail? No! The principle of sowing and reaping doesn't have to work against this generation. God's plan is that sons and daughters will engage in honoring relationships with their parents and that the work of God in one generation can be built upon by the next. When this happens, we'll experience a dramatic increase of God's blessing from generation to generation. In the Bible, Elisha followed the prophet Elijah everywhere he went, honoring and serving him in every way. When God took Elijah to heaven, his mantle fell on Elisha. The Bible says that he received a "double-portion" of Elijah's spirit. I believe this can be the experience of this generation—that children who honor their fathers and mothers will not only build on the platform they leave behind, but experience an increase of what their parents experienced. Played out generation after generation, an entire society can advance into a place of prosperity and fulfillment like the world has never seen.

The practice of honor is essential to your success, and the success of our society. All of these benefits come from simply engaging in honoring relationships. Maybe you've become convinced you'd like to give it a try. Here are some steps to help you move along.

1) **Learn what *honor* really means**
   We've discussed some of the benefits of honor in this chapter, but we haven't gotten to the bottom of what *honor* actually means. In my experience, every person has a different definition. The next chapter breaks honor down and brings clarity to what it's really all about.

2) **Decide which honoring relationships you want to develop**
   At this stage, it's a good idea to make the subject matter of this book more personal. That means applying these concepts to real relationships. Who have you been thinking about as you're reading? A parent? A Pastor? Go ahead and decide on one or two relationships that you want to target

with the practice of honor. Having that in mind will help you process what you're reading.

3) Let honor lead you to action
As you'll discover, honor deals with the heart. But a heart set on honoring will inevitably lead to changes in the way you act. Start preparing yourself now to make changes in your behavior. Chapter 4 shows what honor in action looks like.

CHAPTER THREE

REDEFINING HONOR

The concept of honor is lost on our generation. Even after you recognize the benefits that practicing honor has to offer, it's hard to know where to start. The word *honor* has such a wide variety of meanings. Here are just a few from the dictionary:[1]

personal integrity
to confer a distinction
high or noble rank
in golf, the right to tee off first
in bridge, the ace or one of the top five trump cards
to worship
to accept a method of payment
to salute with a bow

---

[1] honor. Dictionary.com. *Collins English Dictionary - Complete & Unabridged 10th Edition*. HarperCollins Publishers. http://dictionary.reference.com/browse/honor (accessed: June 05, 2013).

It is no wonder people have difficulty understanding and applying honor in relationships! I believe if you can grasp its true meaning, you will find honor much easier to put to practice and you will start receiving its benefits.

The Commandment with an Age Limit?

Turning to the Bible, most people know that *honor* appears in the Fifth of the Ten Commandments: "Honor your father and your mother" (Exodus 20:12). For me, just referencing the Commandments brings back memories of an old Sunday school classroom, a teacher and an ultimatum: Obey your parents or God will not be happy! Perhaps because of that context, I always thought this commandment applied only as long as I was living at home. I figured that as soon as I moved out, I could cross it off the list! What do you think? Does this Commandment pertain only to minors? What about the other Commandments? Were they meant for children or adults? Exploring the Biblical meaning of *honor* reveals an application for adults that many have overlooked.

Let me bore you with just one Hebrew definition. H*onor*, used in the Fifth Commandment, literally means "to make weighty." Imagine a group of wrestlers all lined up in a row, equal in skill, training, and perseverance. Now, in your mind, pick out one and add fifteen pounds of muscle to him. He now stands out from the rest. All other things being equal, as the weightier wrestler, he's likely to win a match against any of the other competitors. He is respected, feared, distinguished. He's unique. He's been given special attention. What I mean by this analogy is that when you decide to honor someone, you "add weight" to their lives. You consider them unique, prefer them, give them special attention, value them, listen to them and respect them. This is the Biblical connotation of honoring your father and mother.

Put Value on Those You Honor

One more boring definition. (Last one, I promise!) This time from the Greek. When New Testament writers reference the Fifth

Commandment, they use the Greek word, *timaō*, which means "fix value on."[2] Let's say you have a penny and you want to honor it. According to the Greek definition, you do so by simply deciding to *fix value* on that penny. You don't care that everyone else believes your penny is virtually worthless. It's worth a lot to you, so you treasure it.

But that's not how most people approach honor. Most people wait until something clearly shows a lot of value. For example, it would be easy to fix value on a $1,000 bill. Its value is already well established, so anyone would "honor" its status and treasure it. Most often, the object of honor must have apparent worth before we place value on it.

However, the Biblical use of "honor" teaches that honoring your father and mother means simply *choosing* to fix value on them. You *put* value on those you honor—whether or not they have earned it or deserve it. Honor isn't contingent on their actions. When you decide to honor someone, you determine that they have worth. You add weight to them in your own frame of reference. You determine "*This person is valuable.*"

Check out this story from the Book of Genesis. Noah's son, Ham, finds his father naked and drunk in his tent. Ham dishonored his father by telling his brothers, so that they could all make fun of Noah together. Ham's brothers chose to honor their father and covered his body. They went so far as to make sure that they didn't even see him, walking backwards with a blanket toward him. (Gen. 9:21-23) Clearly, this was not Noah's shining moment. Though his actions that day were not worthy of honor, two of his sons purposed in their hearts to honor their father anyway. They covered up their father's moment of weakness in such a way that even they wouldn't see it.

---

2 *Strong's Exhaustive Concordance: New American Standard Bible.* 1995. Updated ed. La Habra: Lockman Foundation. http://www.biblestudytools.com/concordances/strongs-exhaustive-concordance/.

Scripture encourages you to value your parents, setting them up to be influences in your life, whether or not they deserve it! Seems crazy, right? But, God knows what He's doing. He knows parents and teachers won't be perfect, but He wants you to value them anyway. With children of my own, I'm beginning to see how important this will be for their future. When I mess up, I'll need them to be able to overlook it and still look to me for wisdom and guidance along the way. If they don't, they'll miss out on the good stuff I actually do have to offer them.

Three Misconceptions About Honor

1) Honor is For Minors

The commandment to honor does not expire with age. Fortunately, neither do the benefits. In fact, they grow richer as you grow older. You can initiate the Honor Cycle at any age by choosing to put value on other people.

2) Honor is Earned

You don't have to wait till people are perfect before they earn your honor. Value your parents simply for being your parents, with no conditions. Withholding honor, even for legitimate reasons, only isolates you from the blessing that practicing honor brings. You may have serious reservations about placing any value on your imperfect parents. But honor may actually help! Check out Chapter Six.

3) Honor is an Action

This is an important distinction. Honor is not an action. Honor is a decision of the heart. It will produce action, but at its core, honor is simply deciding that someone else is valuable. More on this in the next paragraph. Chapter Four takes a look at the actions that honor will produce.

Investigate My Heart

Honor begins with a heart decision to add value to a person. You have to start there, because true honor may look different depending on the situation. At one point, my mom decided to remove her mother's access to her own bank accounts. Looking at this fact in isolation, it might appear that my mom had been disrespectful and dishonoring. But when I supply the context (that my grandmother had dementia and had been swindled by crooks multiple times), my mom's heart of true honor and love becomes apparent. Before launching into actions that seem to conform to some concept of honor, it's helpful to step back and assess the condition of your heart.

I like to ask myself, "Am I holding my father in a place of value? Do I prefer my mother over myself and others?" If you focus only on actions, it's possible to do and say the right things but never come to a place of truly honoring someone. But when your heart is engaged and postured correctly, true honor opens the door for fulfilling relationships with your parents.

<u>WHERE CAN I APPLY THIS STUFF?</u>

These principles work in many relationships, not just between a parent and a child. Scripture asks us to give honor to widows, pastors and elders, employers, governmental leaders, wives, even all people. (See 1 Tim. 5-6 and 1 Peter 2-3.) As you read further, think about how you can experience the benefits of honor in relationships with others in addition to your parents.

I'm Not Only the Author, I'm a Client!
I've always held a pretty good external appearance of honor toward my parents and other figures of authority. Growing up, I learned quickly how to say and do the right things. My mom still tells me that she never considered me to be dishonoring. But I know in my heart that I've struggled over the years with believing that I know best about pretty much everything. I've even approached spirituality with a strong undertow of dishonor. For example, you should know that my parents are some of the most God-loving people I know. They've committed to live holy lives that honor God. They've been faithful to each other and to raising a God-fearing family. They've served in their church my entire life, supporting the work that God is doing there. They've stood against empty religion and sought to share with others the genuine, life-changing relationship that God has given them. They use their gifts and their talents to help others find a deeper, more meaningful relationship with God.

But had run into me the summer before I went to college and asked me about my parents, you would have thought that I was being raised by faithless, compromising, religious wannabes who didn't know the first thing about a real relationship with God. In the midst of true revival in my own life, I stopped looking to my parents as sources of guidance and wisdom. Over the years, I've realized the many areas in which I have not benefited from their input, but instead tried to chart my own course.

Honor is Counter-Cultural
Western culture celebrates the value of independence and self-reliance. It's almost perceived a weakness to seek out advice and support from others, especially parents. Our society makes fun of children who live at home past high school and disdains the success of those who build on platforms they've inherited. In my own life, there have been times in which I didn't value anything that I hadn't earned on my own. "A real man provides for himself," I would

think. Maybe you can relate. I still struggle to place the same value on what I can learn from my parents, teachers and from my pastor as what I can come up with on my own. The truth, though, is that each generation shouldn't be starting from scratch. I appreciate the confidence that comes from nurturing independence in children, but I'm also learning the importance of making sure we value other people, especially those God has commanded us to honor.

CHAPTER FOUR

HONOR IN ACTION

N ow you understand that honor is a decision to place value on another person. That kind of decision, though, must result in some action. You can expect that your behavior is going to change. So what kind of actions will follow?

One application most people are familiar with is that young children should obey their parents. When children decide to honor their parents, they will do what their parents ask them to do. We see this in the Bible when the writer of Ephesians exhorts children to obey their parents. (Eph. 6:1-2) As children grow older, honoring actions may take varying forms.

Two Very Different Applications

Jesus takes the same concept of honor in the Book of Mark and provides two very different applications. This one example from Scripture demonstrates divergent different methods of displaying honor.

> "For Moses said, 'Honor your mother and father'; and,
> 'He who speaks evil of father or mother is to be put to

death.' But you say that if anyone declares that what might have been used to help their father or mother *Corban* (that is, devoted to God)—then you no longer let them do anything for their father or mother. Thus you nullify the word of God by your tradition that you have handed down" (Mark 7:10-13).

Jesus's first admonition is somewhat familiar to our cultural concept of honor. He indicates that we dishonor our father or mother when we speak evil about them. The Old Testament scripture He quotes suggests that a person who speaks evil about his parents should be put to death. Ouch! That strikes me as pretty harsh at first glance. However, the same consequences apply to violations of the other Ten Commandments, so at least we can say God is consistent! Regardless, if we truly hold someone in a place of value and respect, we hold our tongue and don't speak ill of them.

WHAT IF I'VE ALREADY MESSED UP?

For those who are worried about being struck dead for every evil thing you've ever said about your parents (or for the other commandments), there more to the story. We're all in the same boat—worthy of death. But God loved us too much to just sit back and kill us off. He provided a way for us to avoid the penalty of death and live eternal lives in right standing with Him through Jesus. He also provides His Spirit to those who believe in Jesus to help them obey His Commandments and live the best lives possible. Flip to "Empowerment to Live It" toward the end for more details.

As for the second application, it took me a little while to uncover what Jesus was saying. According to Jesus, the Pharisees and the Scribes have prevented people from obeying the Fifth Commandment. How did they do this? They taught that if people gave their money to the Temple that they were no longer obligated to financially support their aging parents. Jesus said that this tradition invalidated the Word of God. In this application, Jesus equates honor with financial support. He shows that true value for fathers and mothers means providing for them financially, perhaps even looking to their financial security before giving consideration to your own.

Several years ago, my sister and her husband did some missions work in some former Soviet states. She described to me a truly disturbing scene from her experience:

> *"In the former Soviet Republic of Kazakhstan, the governmental structures of care for impoverished persons are lacking because of the overall lack of finances in the country. Many people lack means to survive, and the government is unwilling or unable to step in to help. One of the most disheartening aspects of the poverty is a disregard for the elderly. We met one babushka (grandmother) who came from a small village where she had a house and had raised her daughter. She was now unable to work because of her age. Her daughter was working, but her income was barely enough to provide for her and her two children. Hence, the daughter had taken over the house and abandoned the grandmother to her own fate. We found the grandmother in a temporary house set up by a Christian ministry."*

This story is common all over that impoverished country. These are the kind of extremes Jesus was trying to avoid. He advocated a society that values fathers and mothers, both in the way we speak and with our financial support when needed. These are just two examples of actions that honor may produce.

Honor Changes with Age

New ways to show honor to parents reveal themselves at every stage in life. When I was a child, I believed my parents' sole purpose was to provide and care for me. Now, with young children of my own, I am becoming more and more aware of my own parents as individual human beings. I now perceive that they have their own feelings, desires, and struggles. I have observed some of the challenges they face and learned about things they have had to overcome to get where they are. As I mature, I continually see my parents in a whole new light. With each new understanding comes a new application of honor in our relationship. For instance, when I call home, I try to discipline myself to ask questions about what is going on in my parents' lives instead of just talking about me. A heart of honor causes me to want to hear about their interests, things they're thinking about, and projects they're working on. I am able to honor them in a way that I couldn't even fathom when I was younger. Are you ready to take action?

5 Steps to Move Honor into Action

1) Start with the Heart

I can't stress this enough. True honor starts in the heart. Take the time to really consider where your heart is toward the person you want to honor. Just choosing to do and say the "right" things will not have the same affect. Decide that they are valuable to you and let that conviction drive your choice of action.

2) Consider the Situation

Now that your heart is positioned correctly, take time to analyze the situation from your new perspective. What actions would communicate the most value? What actions would position you to receive from what they have to offer? Are there bigger issues as play? Could your actions harm the person you value or enable them to harm themselves? Honorable actions will look different in every unique situation.

3) **Weigh your own motivations**

Making decisions that honor other people is not natural. Most people are used to putting their own interests and motivations before others. Because of this, you'll want to think through how your personal interests are motivating your actions. Will an honorable action cost you time, emotional energy or resources? Will it force you to deal with an unpleasant memory or lingering unforgiveness? Don't skip over your own interests. Identify them and chose to lay them down in honor of another person.

4) **Choose an honoring action**

Now it's time to make a commitment. Choose the action that puts them first and truly values the person you want to honor. For practical ideas that may apply to your situation, check out the list ideas toward the end.

5) **Go for it!**

All that's left to do now is act on your commitment. Don't stop short of this step! Although the heart is the starting point for true honor, actions are the fruit. Make sure that your honor is being displayed through actions. The Bible says, "faith by itself, if it is not accompanied by action, is dead" (James 2:17). Similarly, honor without action is pointless. Communicate honor in your words and actions and start seeing the benefits of the Honor Cycle flowing your way!

It really is that simple. You may find, however, that putting these simple steps to action is not all that easy. There are some stumbling blocks you'll need to hurdle.

<u>WHAT IF PRACTICING HONOR IS TOO DIFFICULT?</u>

I recognize that honoring actions are not always easy to choose. I watched my mom and dad both selflessly give so much energy in the final months of their parents' lives. I marveled at the way they continually denied themselves to serve my grandparents. One thing that kept them going was the awareness that it was only a season of their lives. They chose to honor their parents through a difficult season. That season ended, and now honor takes a much different form. I hope that will encourage you. Honor may call you to extreme measures at times, but one day you'll look back from a new season, proud of your honorable actions.

Two Stumbling Blocks

In my experience, young people today have difficulty understanding honor. When a principle like this one gets lost over a period of time, future generations will stumble over it. It's not always out of deliberate disobedience. Rather, because they are so far removed from the principle, they cannot even wrap their minds around it. An Old Testament verse says, "Repent and turn away from all your transgressions, so that iniquity may not become a stumbling block to you" (Ezek. 18:30, NASB).

The root word for *iniquity* means to bend, twist, or distort.[1] Iniquity results when we are bent the wrong way. We may think we're doing it right when we're actually dead wrong. Imagine a ship with a bent rudder. You can push the tiller the right way,

---

[1] *Strong's Exhaustive Concordance: New American Standard Bible.* 1995. Updated ed. La Habra: Lockman Foundation. http://www.biblestudytools. com/concordances/strongs-exhaustive-concordance/.

but the ship won't go where you want it to go. That's how the principle of honor is working against this generation. I genuinely believe that people desire to be someone who honors. (After all, who would ever admit that they want to dishonor people around them?) The problem isn't with the intention to honor, but with two factors that cause honor's true meaning and application to be misunderstood: false examples of honor and an overemphasis on expressing feelings.

False Examples of Honor

Honor is primarily associated with actions instead of the heart, so this generation has concluded that honor is simply obedience, speaking respectfully or withholding an opinion in deference to another. This is the kind of action-based honor that has been demonstrated by previous generations. It looks like this:

- A kid who says "yes, sir" to his father, but despises him in his heart
- An employee who represses his ideas to avoid a confrontation with his boss
- A wife who submits to emotional abuse in reverence to her husband
- A cultist who blindly follows a leader to his death

These are people hiding behind cloaks of "honor." This perverted idea of honor has been paraded as the real deal. For the most part, nobody buys it anymore, and rightly so! A deceitful display of honor only leads to emotional hurt. It leaves you feeling powerless and often causes you to hurt others. You sense that this is not what true honor is about. As a result you may have fled in the opposite direction. Hopefully Chapter 3 has helped you redefine honor and given you a better perspective.

Focus on Expressing Feelings

The second stumbling block is a surge of teaching focused on the need to express true feelings and emotions. Undoubtedly, you've heard that suppressing your feelings can result in psychological trauma, and you've been taught to express what's going on inside. The growing consensus dictates that you should be "real" and upfront with your opinions and emotions. Our culture challenges you to unapologetically present who you really are instead of putting on a façade.

Not long ago, I had a meeting with someone serving in a department that I led. I barely knew her and expected that she would want to use the time to learn more about me, the church, or the department we were serving in. Instead, she used the time to express ways in which I was misleading the department, offer criticism of me and other members of our team, and suggest how we might do a better job. I try to remain open to constructive comments, but this conversation was disrespectful and hurtful. She had shoved a litany of opinions in my face without any attempt to soften the blow. I'll never forget the way she ended our time together. She closed by saying, "I'm sorry if I seem a bit rude or upfront, but I'm just not someone who's going to be fake and hide my true feelings." Pondering that conversation and many others just like it, I realized that she truly believed that she was doing the right thing by speaking to me that way.

Let me be quick to point out that I don't disagree with our need to be honest about our feelings. Tucking things away in the heart and never expressing them tears you apart from the inside and can ruin you and the people you love. People must learn to be honest with themselves and others in order to mature emotionally. Here's the problem. Focusing solely on the need to emote compromises your ability to engage other people in a loving way. The communication is one-sided and often hurtful, not to mention dishonoring.

Honest and Honoring

So how can you express your feelings honestly, yet in a way that honors the listener? By now it should come as no surprise to you that the answer begins in the heart!

Last year, I met with a young adult at our church to discuss an email he had sent to our Senior Pastor. I wanted to help this young man see how the tone of his email was hurtful and dishonoring. He explained to me that he believed the most honoring thing that he could do was to share his feelings in a straightforward manner, in the same way he would to a peer or friend. In his mind, he would do our Pastor a disservice by toning down his harsh rhetoric. "If the Pastor needs me to sugar-coat my comments, what does that say about him? If I assume he needs me to do that, what does that say about what I think about him?"

This young man was missing the point. By sharing his feelings in "the same way he would to a peer or friend," he demonstrated that he placed no special value on the relationship with his pastor. Honor is not about catering to the emotional needs of others, but rather making an effort in every communication to value, respect and give weight to their position. When you value someone, you communicate with them as if they are special. It's okay to give them the special treatment. Actually, that's the point!

A Difficult Conversation

With a correct perspective on honor, we can be both honest and honoring at the same time. A friend of mine once had to have a difficult conversation with her mom. She explained, "One time, at a particularly trying time of her life, I noticed that my mom's negativity was spreading in dangerous ways. Her anger was pushing away the relationships that she held dear." My friend, like many of her family members, had been personally hurt and offended by her mom's outbursts of anger. She quickly came to the realization, though, that focusing on her own need to emote would not help her mother or be an honorable way to approach the conversation. "To reach my mother, I had to move beyond my first response of offense at her anger and speak the truth in love."

You can be honest and forthright about your feelings and emotions and still keep a posture that honors. It may take special care, thought, and a greater time commitment, but your willingness to do that will go a long way in communicating honor to your parents.

Tips for Being Honest and Honoring

- Set aside adequate time for communication.
- Be willing to invest emotional energy.
- Calm down. Deal with your anger and offense first.
- Don't make negative assumptions about motives.
- Communicate respectfully.
- Seek to Understand them before being Understood.
- Communicate how their actions make you feel, not how they need to change.
- Ask permission before giving critical feedback. Also consider that it may not be your place to give feedback.

CHAPTER FIVE

DOES HONOR ALWAYS MEAN OBEDIENCE?

A girl from my high school came from a privileged family. However, Debbie (not her real name) had a difficult transition into adulthood. Her mother was plagued with an unrealistic fear that Debbie would never find a spouse. This fear drove Debbie's mom to control every decision Debbie made from 18-years-old on from a warped point of view. Her mother used emotional pressure to influence Debbie about her choice in college, what kind of car she drove, how she did her hair, her weight, her clothing, her friends, even her spiritual beliefs. When Debbie resisted her, her mother began to put pressure on her to come back home where it would be easier to make sure she was positioned to marry well. What should Debbie have done? Her mother's motives were clearly imbalanced. How could Debbie take on a posture of honor?

Honor and Obedience

This is going to be hard to accept, but I propose that whatever the circumstance, parents can and should be honored. Honor is essential, even when undeserved. Without it, children miss out on all of the benefits we've talked about. And, as we'll see, one of a parent's deepest needs goes unmet. However, honor doesn't always mean blind obedience. In fact, honor and obedience are separate ideas. Honor is a heart condition that may lead to the action of obedience, but sometimes leads to other actions.

Young Children
As a young child, a heart of honor will almost always lead you to obey your parents. Under their guardianship, you're not responsible for many of your actions; your parents are, and your responsibility is to listen and obey. That's one reason the scripture clearly states, "Children, obey your parents in everything" (Col. 3:20, Eph. 6:1). As young children, the only appropriate time to disobey parents is when they ask us to disobey God's Word. Even in these rare instances, it is possible to take an honoring posture.

Growing Older
Let's get real, though. Most of you live on our own. You might even have children of your own. You're accountable for your own choices. What does honor mean for you? As you matured, you and your parents worked together over time, transferring more and more responsibility to you, removing them from accountability for many of your actions. During and after this process, you may still honor your parents, though not always with blind obedience. I think about my responsibility as a father. I'm fully accountable for how my children grow and develop. Because of that, I eagerly seek the advice and counsel of my parents on childrearing. My wife and I do the same with her parents. We put great weight on their input and we value it so much.

At the end of the day, Eileen and I are responsible for raising our children, and we make final decisions that may or may not line up exactly with the advice we've been given. Yet we maintain a posture of honor. When we do it right, we intentionally seek out advice and weigh it heavily in the decision-making process. We sow honor even when the final decision rests with us. A friend of mine put it this way: "Ultimately, I am responsible to God for my decisions. As an adult, I can't say 'but my dad told me to...' or 'but Pastor told me to....' When I make a major life decision, I make sure that my parents and mentors understand that I value and give weight to their input, even if I don't follow it."

Honoring While Being Accountable for Your Decisions:

- Seek out advice.
- Really try to understand that advice.
- Ask lots of questions.
- Compare and contrast points of view in open dialogue.
- Leave an open door for further input.

Submissive Relationships

When you become an adult and are accountable for your own decisions, you may find there are still areas of your life that you should submit to others in obedience. In those cases, how do you know whether the honoring response is to obey or to simply give weight to the person's advice? In every instance, first make sure your heart is set to honor and then carefully decide how to respond. Here are two questions to help you determine whether honor requires obedience:

1) Who bears responsibility for the actions you will take?
2) Has God asked you to submit this area of your life to this person?

Who Bears Responsibility?

For instance, if an employer asks you to do a certain task relating to the company, even if you don't like it, honoring his or her position as your employer would mean not only being respectful in your response, but also being obedient to carry out the request. In this situation, your employer is the responsible authority in the work environment, not you. This holds true for relationships with all kinds of authorities—church leadership, government, teachers, homeowners association board, e.g. In their respective realms, they are responsible for you and your actions. Within those realms, you honor them by being both obedient and respectful. Scripture says that every person is to be subject to these governing authorities, because God puts them in place. When we resist them, we resist Him. (Rom. 13:1-4)

Has God Asked You to Submit?

Even when you're ultimately responsible for certain choices, there are times that you will enter into relationships in which you temporarily defer to others. In those situations, honor may mean being obedient to others even when they're not ultimately responsible for your actions. For instance, if you engage a personal trainer to help you become physically fit, you'd be wise to obey what they ask of you, even when you don't feel like it or understand why. You've deferred to them because of their expertise in a particular area. You're probably not going to obey their financial advice, but you'll go against your own will to obey them in the gym.

You may engage in this kind of relationship with a parent, pastor, mentor, accountability partner or someone who is apprenticing you. It may be temporary over just a little area of your life, or a long-term relationship that spans many areas of influence. The key here is that while you are still responsible for your life and choices, you've decided to obey someone else in certain areas. I find God will ask me to engage in these types of relationships from time to time.

One such occasion came just before I was about to ask Eileen to marry me. It was very important to me that her father give his approval before we became engaged. Some may find this old-fashioned, but I believe there are times when honoring the right people at the right time can bring a greater degree of God's blessing. Honoring her father in this instance was taking the next step of our relationship and submitting it to him. Eileen and I were both out of the house, both very responsible for our own lives and choices, but we were committed to submit this decision to him. So, Eileen's father, Peter, and I arranged to meet at the local Starbucks to talk about the pending engagement.

Honestly, at first I thought the whole process was more of a formality than anything. It hadn't occurred to me that he might not think it was a good idea! I don't think I'll ever forget standing in Starbucks, the engagement ring tucked away in a box in my back pocket, dazed, wondering what had just happened. I had imagined that conversation ending with a couple of slaps on the back as we admired the ring together. But the ring never came out of that pocket and my hopes of a Christmas engagement were dashed. It turned out that Peter had a different perspective on the maturity of our relationship and wanted to see us walk through a couple of more seasons together before committing to marriage.

Looking back, I can completely understand his point of view, but that news wasn't easy to take at the time. Nevertheless, I was fully prepared in my heart to wait until we had his permission to move forward in our relationship. Honoring Peter as Eileen's father meant obedience. A short while later, he gave his blessing, and I'm so thankful for the role he plays in our lives to this day as a father, mentor, confidant and friend.

How to Honor when not Obeying

Depending on the answer to these two questions, honor may mean simple obedience to the parent or person you've determined to honor. However, if the person is *not* a governing authority and God has *not* asked you to submit an area of your life to them, honor may take a different form. In those cases lean heavily on the Biblical meaning of honor, i.e. "to put value on" or "to make weighty." When I get it right, the input of someone I desire to honor, weighs heavily in my decision-making. I seek out their advice and make efforts to truly understand it. Then after I've respectfully considered it and dialogued with them, I either gratefully act on it or gracefully set it aside. This process takes time and commitment to the relationship, but will usually result in parents being honored and feeling respected, even if their suggestion is not implemented.

Going back to my friend Debbie's story, she decided not to move back home, despite her mother's wishes. She recognized that she could not allow her mother's fear to control her decision and that she had to take responsibility for her choice about where to live. She took the time, though, to travel home and discuss the choice with her parents. In fact, she dedicated a summer to travel with her parents, making sure they were a part of the decision and carefully listening to their input. The decision was hard on her mom, but the relationship is intact and her mother knows that Debbie cherishes and appreciates her perspective.

As another illustration, some married friends of mine recently considered a real estate purchase. They were very excited about the possibility of becoming homeowners and had settled on a property to invest in. They wisely sought the advice of their parents on both sides. Through the process they realized that their excitement about the property had overshadowed some real structural issues that would affect the long-term value of the investment. Honoring their parents by involving them in the discussion and weighing their advice was difficult because they were somewhat emotionally attached to the property. In the end, they chose to accept the input and decided not to purchase, which was likely a very wise decision. Whether choosing to implement the suggestions of parents or not, it's the posture of honor that matters. If you maintain that honoring posture, you'll see great benefits throughout your life.

CHAPTER SIX

WHAT HONOR DOES FOR PARENTS

I don't think of myself as a needy person. But, if I'm honest with myself, I recognize my emotional needs. You would think that in my relationships with my children that it would be all give and no take. While there are moments where that is true, I'm finding that parenting is just like any other relationship. I have a role in giving, but I also have needs from the relationship. I need to feel respected. I need to know that my life is making a difference and that I have an enduring legacy in my children. I don't let those needs drive the relationship, but when they're met, it helps me become a much better parent. When my children assume a posture of honor, it not only positions them for blessing, it meets a significant need in me. Moreover, when my children honor me, they bring out my best parenting, which fulfills their needs as well.

An Unlikely Source of Counsel

I once had a friend stay with me for a few months in my DC home. He had moved to the area, because he and his girlfriend, who worked in DC, were taking their relationship to the next level. He wanted to be close so they could spend more time together growing as a couple. As their relationship progressed, it was important to them that they involve her father in the process. The problem was that she didn't have the best relationship with her dad. He hadn't been the best role model for her, was rarely present, and didn't share her values. His girlfriend wasn't sure how it would turn out, but they agreed together to involve him in their relationship. He reported, "When we set to honor her dad by including him in our relationship, at first he was very abrasive. But in the long run, it was extremely healing for both sides." Not only did their relationship improve, but the demand on him to step into this role pulled the best out of him and helped him become a better father. Now this couple is married with kids, and they enjoy a fulfilling relationship with her father.

Honor is Love

Jesus said that all of the Law hangs on these two commandments: 1) love God, and 2) love others. (Matt. 22:37-40) This really gets me thinking. Every command in the Bible is actually an expression of love, including the Fifth Commandment to honor your father and mother. Honor is not only for your own benefit; it's the best way that you can love your parents. As you grow older, you start to experience all kinds of different relationships. You realize that in every type of relationship there are ways to give and receive love. Spouses love each other one way, siblings in another, and best friends in yet another way. Students love their teachers. Pastors love their congregants. Husbands love their in-laws. For each type of relationship love carries a different expression. The expression is determined by the physical and emotional needs that drive the relationship.

I'm realizing that one of the primary needs that parents have from their children is to be honored. Perhaps the most damaging thing that I can do emotionally to my parents is to no longer consider them valuable, i.e., to dishonor them. A friend of mine who spent some time working for the Health and Aging Program at the Pan-

American Health Organization told me the results of an interesting study. The study showed that dishonor and lack of appreciation from children is extremely hurtful to older adults, in some cases leading to suicidal thoughts. I'm not surprised by its findings. A heart of dishonor wounds a parent in a way that actions alone never could. Children can disobey, argue and even become physically violent with their parents, and these things might do far less damage than simply deciding that their parents don't matter to them anymore.

For most people, whatever esteem their children hold them in will become their only lasting legacy. To watch your children demote you to just another person and remove you from that pedestal in their heart is to watch your own legacy reduced to dust. Parents need to know that their children value them and hold a special place for them in their hearts. I don't mean to make parents sound weak and needy. They're not. They're no weaker than a husband who needs respect or a wife who needs affection. We all have needs from various relationships, and honor is what parents need from a healthy relationship with their children.

Honor Draws Out the Best
Even as a young parent, when my need for honor is met, it pulls the best out of me. When my daughter asks me questions about God and relationships, and I sense that her heart is wide open to learn from me, I get serious about what I say. I don't take it lightly. I know that my words are shaping the belief system of another person. It's a big responsibility. Many times I have to analyze my own motives and beliefs to make sure I'm giving the best answers to her questions about life. I think this is a universal response of healthy parenting. While dishonor may cause a wounded parent to exert control and irrational behavior toward a child, honor will often cause them to take a new posture. When children communicate that they value their parents, want to learn from them, and want their parents to have input into their lives, parents will rise to the challenge.

They'll start weighing their own motivations and thought processes, searching for jewels of wisdom to pull from their own journey. Dishonor may cause parents to live defensively about the choices they've made, but honor will cause them to examine their choices and help their children make better ones. When parents feel secure that they are valued, the weight of that position will drive them to be the best parents (role-models, advisors, confidants) they can be.

Honor and Forgiveness

For some, I know this whole subject is incomprehensible. One or both of your parents were abusive or absent and you can't even imagine talking to them for more than five seconds, much less putting value on them or letting them weigh in on big decisions in your life. I can't pretend to understand your pain or know how difficult it must be to consider all this. Honestly, I admire you just for reading this far into the book. I don't know the pain you feel. I do know that true healing can take place in your own heart as you let go of hurt and release forgiveness. Jesus made a strong case for forgiveness when he challenged us to extend the same mercy to others that God has extended to us. It is not easy, especially when the wounds are painful and deep. However, the truth is that withholding forgiveness only ensures that hurt will never heal.

The first step to honor may simply mean accepting that your parents are human, imperfect, and wounded by relationships with their own parents or others. Then, release forgiveness toward them. Even the most hurtful parents are still parents in need of honor from their children. Maybe a forgiving, honoring child is the catalyst that will begin healing in their heart and help shape them into a better parent.

Part One – Summary:

- Honor is a Commandment with a promise. Honor your parents, and you will experience amazing benefits.
- Honor starts in the heart with a decision to put value on someone.
- Honor will lead to action. The application of honor will look different in every situation.
- It is possible to be both Honest and Honoring.
- Honor doesn't always lead to obedience. They are separate ideas.
- Honor not only benefits you, it meets one of the deepest felt needs of your parents.

Most important of all, honor initiates the Honor Cycle in your relationships. As you practice honor, you'll open the door to receive something very valuable that your parents can release to you—their Blessing!

PART TWO: RELEASING THE BLESSING

Young adults are in a unique position. Many of you, like me, not only have relationships with living parents or parental figures, you also have young children of your own. Or, perhaps you're considering starting a family in the next few years. The Honor Cycle works synergistically among generations. You have the opportunity to initiate the cycle in two directions: first, by practicing honor toward your parents, and then by purposefully releasing a blessing over your children.

Blessing sounds to me like such a spiritual thing. And while it is deeply spiritual, it doesn't have to be that far-out of a concept. One of the first recorded blessings was actually from God, when he first created Man.

> *"God blessed them and said to them, "Be fruitful and increase in number; fill the earth and subdue it. Rule over the fish of the sea and the birds of the sky and over every creature thing that moves on the ground."*
>
> Genesis 1:28

Like this charge from God, blessings are simply words that come from the heart and speak identity and purpose over another person. When those words are inspired by God and received by the hearer, they have power to shape the future.

Biblically, the blessing of a parent is extremely special. In his final moments, Jacob lined up his children and blessed each of them. (Gen. 49) His words became accurate predictions of their future. When the writer of Hebrews referenced this moment, he used the Greek word *eulogeo* for the blessing that Jacob gave. (Heb. 11:29) I love this definition of that word: "to cause to prosper."[1] When you speak words of blessing over your children, you set them up to prosper in every realm of life!

Releasing the Blessing is the other side of the Honor Cycle. It works hand in hand with *Practicing Honor* to empower generations to build a more prosperous future, one on the other.

Here's What You'll Need to Get Started

1) **Understand the Power of Your Blessing**
   The Bible says, "The tongue has the power of life and death" (Prov. 18:21). The words you speak over your children have a tremendous impact. In the next chapter I expose the power in a simple blessing.

2) **Separate the Behavior from their Identity**
   You probably understand your responsibility as a parent to correct inappropriate behavior. What you may not know is that these moments are ripe with opportunity to bless (or curse) your child. Chapter 8 will help you learn to correct behavior and release a blessing at the same time.

---

1 *Strong's Exhaustive Concordance: New American Standard Bible.* 1995. Updated ed. La Habra: Lockman Foundation. http://www.biblestudytools.com/concordances/strongs-exhaustive-concordance/.

3) Let God Empower Your Blessing

Chances are that blessing was not perfectly modeled for you as a child. That doesn't have to be a setback. Faith in God is the perfect remedy, both as a model of blessing and as a source of empowerment. Check out Chapter 9.

4) Let the Blessing Flow!

I've learned that you don't have to be conservative with your blessing. I've included at the end a list of 30 practical ideas on how to release a blessing. Start practicing today!

CHAPTER SEVEN

THE POWER OF A SIMPLE BLESSING

I kicked my feet up into the nose of my mom's Chevy Lumina mini-van as I reclined in the passenger seat. Mom listened intently as I divulged my most recent plan to take over the world. (I did almost all my dreaming out loud in the days before my dad taught me that I could think before opening my mouth.) Mom always actively participated in these sessions, asking questions, probing my logic, supporting my conclusions and offering her own creative contributions. During these sessions, I conceived a vision of some academic and extra-curricular achievements that I eventually accomplished. I talked about relational goals, student leadership opportunities, business ideas, and plans for the future. Doubtless, I said crazy, nonsensical things bordering on the impossible or self-centered things rooted in faulty motives. Regardless, I never left that mini-van feeling discouraged about the dreams in my heart. On the contrary, I eagerly headed inside to plan out my next move, knowing I could do anything in my heart. In a simple way, I had been blessed. My mom had affirmed me and the dreams in my heart and empowered me to succeed in whatever I set out to do.

Words of Affirmation

I've struggled over the years with the idea of speaking blessings over others. It's a behavior that just doesn't come natural to me. At all. Yet God has a sense of humor, because He paired me with a spouse who feels most loved when she receives words of affirmation. Holding her hand, hanging out together, and buying her gifts are nice, but having the perfect supportive words at the right time is what really makes her feel loved. This made for an interesting dating relationship. Not wanting to come up short when needing to offer a supportive word, I picked up a notepad and titled it "Words of Affirmation." Every time I thought of a good verbal affirmation or something that would make her feel loved, I would write it down in the notepad. I always kept my notepad on hand in case I needed a quick word. The interesting thing is that I started to see how these words built her up, gave her confidence, and reminded her of the awesome potential inside of her. She knew about the notebook (I may have even read out of it on occasion), but the words of blessing were nevertheless impactful. Blessings are a great power in the hands of one who wields them. It can change the course of someone's life, release their hidden potential, and empower them for decades.

On a recent visit to my parents' home in South Carolina, I had the opportunity to ask them a question that had puzzled me for months. You see, at several key moments in my teenage years I made good choices to avoid traps that ensnared many of my friends. Looking back on those choices, I realized that my ability to resist peer pressure stemmed from a deep-rooted belief that I was special. I genuinely believed that I was created to do bigger, better things, and thus had a higher standard to uphold than those around me. Notwithstanding the obvious arrogance, this idea served me well throughout adolescence. Now, with young children of my own, I needed to know where the belief came from. I sat down with my mom and dad and asked them, "How did you raise me to believe that

I was special?" My dad shrugged his shoulders, rubbed his mustache and said, "I seem to remember when you were pretty young telling you that you were special, that you were gifted."

At first, I thought, "That's it?! You just said it?!" Then I started thinking about all of the little things that people have "just said" that have vividly shaped my self-image. One time my grandmother saw me running and suggested I try out for the track team. I never got around to it, but have believed since that day that I could have been a track star. My grandfather told me I could pay my way through college using my talent as a square dance caller. I held on to that as a back-up career for almost a decade. My dad was once impressed with an analogy I used when I pretended to preach a sermon as a kid, so I figured I might become a preacher. A voice teacher told me that if I worked hard, I could make a living singing. I still dream about taking two years off work to star on Broadway. A Nordstrom sales associate liked the gift I bought for my wife and told me I was a good husband. I went for two weeks thinking about how lucky my wife is to have me. Looking back, I started to realize that the power of even a simple blessing is astounding!

Despite all the words of blessing spoken over me, I started my adult life without understanding its power. I just didn't see the point. In fact, I felt that people would benefit more from a dose of sarcastic criticism than they would from any positive words. I figured, why go around inflating people's egos if I had the opportunity to make them aware of their shortcomings? I thought that life and ministry were about building something great—a great organization, a great system, a great spiritual movement. The people involved were expendable for this mission. Quite frankly, people without a sense of self-worth seemed easier to control. As I reflect back over those years, I realize that my words were not only absent of blessing, they were full of curses, tearing apart people's self-image and the dreams in their heart.

Slowly, my perspective began to change. It started as I reflected on my Pastor's constant reminder: "Ministry is people." He explained that you can't separate the work we're doing from the people involved in the work: "We're not building a ministry; we're building people." I began to redefine success. Rather than trying to use the people around me to accomplish the mission, I started using the mission as a rally point to build up people. I started deliberately speaking words of blessing over people around me and immediately noticed a huge difference in their response. The same power that I had used to tear others down was now building people up. Those simple words began working more change for good in their lives than my criticism ever did.

A great friend of mine has an amazing story of the power of the blessing. When he was young, he struggled with a learning disability. It was so severe that his teachers recommended he be placed in a school for the mentally challenged. They doubted whether he would ever be able to read and write. But his parents didn't treat him like he was challenged. They constantly affirmed the brilliance that they could see inside him. Despite evidence to the contrary, they spoke to him and interacted with him as one with full intellectual capacity. The inner-image that his parents spoke into his life eventually dominated the disability. He may have worked harder than others, but he grew into that person that his parents always believed he was. Eventually, he became the President of a non-profit organization that feeds hundreds of thousands of children every day in Africa. He's also one of the most brilliant communicators I know.

Words are Seeds

"I've seen some real potential in you and I want to get you involved as a partner in my business." It took me ten years to realize that this sentence is the opening line of the sales pitch for just about all multi-level marketing opportunities. Even now that I know it's just part of a sales pitch, I am still occasionally enticed into a small group meeting with other unsuspecting observers. I can't resist those powerful words: "I've seen some real potential in you." I hadn't even graduated from high school before two people dropped that line on me for two different multi-level marketing companies. And they had me—hook, line and sinker! This simple sentence of blessing had power to build an image on the inside of me.

How does that work? How can words be so powerful? It really is fascinating. It seems it's just the way God designed things. After all, He created the entire universe with His words! (Gen. 1) When my daughter was just born, I started thinking about words as seeds. It seemed appropriate because Jesus compares the Word of God to a seed in His parables. (Luke 8:11) I started to visualize my words entering Audrey's heart and producing fruit—in the form of an internal image. Eventually, this image would emerge for all to see. Words of blessing would produce good fruit, while negative words would produce bad fruit. I started to believe that you can look at the fruit of a person's life and trace it back to seeds (words) that were planted at some point along the way. And while every person has the power to decide which seeds they want to water and nourish to fruition, an onslaught of negativity and a lack of blessing will set any child behind, especially if they never find a source of blessing to counter the negative images developing on the inside.

HELP! I'VE BEEN THE VICTIM OF NEGATIVE WORDS!

If you've had negative words spoken over you, you're not doomed to live out those words. God, who spoke the first blessing over man, continues to speak words of blessing over His creation. The Bible is full of God's words over you. You can chose to receive those words and reject the negative words of hurtful people. God's words will reshape your inner-image and begin building His picture of the future on the inside of you!

What Seeds Are You Sowing?

Have you ever thought about yourself as a prophet in your own household? A prophet speaks God-inspired words about the future, and those words come to pass. What kind of future are your words producing in your children? When I began thinking this way, I could hardly go out in public without shuddering at the images being painted on the inside of children: "Bad boy!" "What's wrong with you?!" "You're so annoying!" "You're going to grow up to be a bum!" Sadly, in these cases, what I see in public is likely just the tip of the iceberg. What happens at home when the report card arrives from school, when heated disputes erupt, when chores don't get done right, when little boys don't put in the right effort in sports, or when young girls get caught eating junk food? If words are seeds, and children are fertile soil for words of identity from their parents, it's no wonder the Apostle Paul wrote to the Ephesians: "Do not let any unwholesome talk come out of your mouths, but only what is helpful for building up others according to their needs, that it may benefit those who listen" (Eph. 4:29). What an amazing power given to parents! I look at my two young children, not even in grade school, but full of purpose and vision for their lives. They are special. They are beautiful. They are royal. They are loved. They are anything that God has said about them in His Word. Eileen and I have purposed to affirm God's words about them through our blessing.

CHAPTER EIGHT

WHAT ABOUT CORRECTING
NEGATIVE BEHAVIOR?

I f you have children already, you may be wondering at this point how you're supposed to affirm them *and* discipline them at the same time. Till now we've discussed only the importance of speaking positive words. But if you've been a parent for more than five minutes, you've realized that you can't go around identifying merely good things to say about your children! You often must correct them and address negative aspects of their behavior if you want them to have a healthy, well-adjusted future. Your challenge, as a parent, is to address negative behavior without injecting a negative identity, to always bless without necessarily approving of everything your children do. Here's a key observation I've found: there is a difference between who your children are (identity) and what choices they make (behavior). With my young children, I'm learning to use my language to address these issues separately. In fact, any time they behave *negatively*, I look for the opportunity to affirm a *positive* aspect of their identity. Here's an example from my wife's childhood.

Eileen's behavior didn't always reflect the jewel that she is on the inside. One day after teachers caught her smoking at school, she was preparing for an intense conversation with her dad. But Peter took an interesting approach. Rather than coming down hard on her behavior, he talked to her about the potential he saw in her. He told her that he saw her as a leader and contrasted her behavior with who he knew she really was. Eileen didn't wake up the next day and become a model student, but her father's words stuck with her and began to affect the way she saw herself. That conversation was a turning point for her. Within a year she had corrected a lot of her behavior and was selected by the school faculty and her peers to serve as the head student leader. That one little moment of blessing still affects Eileen today and has helped shape her into an amazing leader. That conversation could have gone a lot differently. Had Peter not separated Eileen's behavior from her identity, he could have said things that would have painted a sad picture of her future. I thank God that, despite her bad behavior, he chose to inspire her rather than deflate her.

Now, your little angels probably don't ever frustrate you. Personally, I have to be careful in moments of frustration to guard my mouth from introducing words of negative identity into my children. Here's something I've been practicing while my kids are young. Before I ever address a behavioral issue, I try to deal with the internal image of them that I'm developing. I make sure it's a positive one and then take intentional steps to communicate it. I hope that with practice I can continue addressing my children's behavior this way as they enter adolescence.

The process I go through with my children is not all that different than what I do as a church leader. When I experience frustration with people in our congregation, it's tempting to start addressing the issue by asking, "What's wrong with these people?!" But the question itself shows that my heart is already in the wrong place. I've already made a negative identity statement about the people whose behavior needs to be addressed, i.e., that they have something wrong with them. If that's the message I communicate, I'll only shoot myself in the foot. The image I paint on the inside of them with my words would be that they're hopeless, that their behavior proves they're dysfunctional. The truth is that they have the seed of God on the inside of them. Each one is a new creation in Christ (2 Cor. 5:17), made in the image of God (Gen. 1:26). If I can get them to identify with the potential of greatness on the inside of them, their behavior will automatically start to change.

When you look beyond the behavior of your children and remind yourself of their God-given potential, it becomes easier to find a starting place to affirm them and help develop the inner-image they see of themselves. Beside the voice of God Himself, a parent's voice is the most powerful voice in a child's life. I know the words of blessing that my parents speak over me continue to have a profound impact on my life. Whether age two or thirty-two, it's never too late in our child's life to start being a voice of blessing that makes a difference.

Believing the Best

It starts so young. My daughter, Audrey, was only two when we found ourselves having to correct her behavior many times a day. She remains a very strong-willed child (which I love), but every day there is a temptation to slip over into assigning her an identity of "disobedient." Separating her behavior from her identity was difficult when she would exhibit such strong evidence of inability to follow instructions. Yet, Eileen and I committed that even if it took years, we would always be surprised if she didn't obey us. I'm not always perfect in living up to that commitment, but ideally, even when Audrey gets out of bed for the fifth time in the same night, I'll still believe in my heart that she is an obedient child.

This belief affects the way I think about her, the way I discipline her and the way I talk to her. When she misbehaves, I reinforce in my communication that I believe she wants to obey, and that this behavior isn't consistent with what I know to be true about her heart. What is the alternative? If I get discouraged and believe that she is a devil sent to torment me when I'm trying to have down time, then my words and my actions will only reinforce that identity. How many children reach their 12th birthday already firmly believing that they are a problem child, a poor academic performer, unattractive, promiscuous, or accident-prone? How much of their self-image is the result of their actions, and how much can be attributed to the reactions and outbursts of parents and parental-figures around them? Words of blessing cannot happen without a choice to believe the best about who someone is, despite their behavior.

The truth is, although their actions greatly differ, people's hearts are good. People have to be pretty messed up to wake up every day thinking, "What can I do today to hurt other people and mess up the world I live in? How can I displease my parents? What kind of trouble can I get in?" That's just not in most people's hearts and intentions. Even if it is there, it's usually in direct contradiction with the true side of them, the person God created them to be. That redemptive side of them has just never been affirmed or developed. Unfortunately, many of us do wake up every day and hurt other people, mess up the world around us, displease our parents and get into all sorts of trouble. We know that we need people close to us who understand our failings and continue to believe the best about us. In the same way, your child needs you to continue to believe the best about them, as they look to you to help shape their own inner-image.

Five Tips for Blessing while Correcting Behavior

1) **Pick the Right Time**
Parenting in public is tough. You know how it feels when your child exhibits negative behavior and people see it. You

can feel the glares of everyone who notices. They expect you to correct your child while they watch and assume that if you don't, you aren't doing it all. But I've found it difficult to take the time and focus to correct every negative behavior in public. Sometimes I just wink at the judgmental cloud of witnesses and wait to address the problem when I have time to speak my blessing and do it the right way. With practice, you may be able to handle situations in public as well. Then you can allow your ego to swell as onlookers marvel at your parenting skills.

2) Get Your Heart Right

The Bible says, "The mouth speaks what the heart is full of" (Matt. 12:34, Luke 6:45). No matter how hard you try, if you believe your child is evil, a blessing is not going to come out of your mouth! Take a pause. Remember how special your child is to you. Remember what God says about them. Ask Him to help you reshape your inner image of your child to match His inner image of them.

3) Choose Your Words Carefully

There is a difference between "Your actions are so inappropriate" and "You are so bad." Make sure the words you choose differentiate between your child's identity (good) and their behavior (not always good).

4) Start with Affirmation

Before addressing the negative behavior, affirm your child's identity. Let them know that you believe their heart is good. I often say to my young children, "I know you want to obey Daddy. I know you want to make my job easy. I so appreciate your heart to obey. Let's talk about your actions, because I don't feel those actions are what you want to do."

Sometimes I don't think even *they* agree with me! But I am affirming the potential I see inside of them, whether they see it or not. What behavior do you want to address? What identity issues could be connected with that behavior? How could you affirm a positive identity?

5) Don't Do It In Your Own Strength

Chances are you are not capable of being a continuous source of blessing for your child on your own. I've found that being intentional about blessing my child often requires more than my natural ability. In the next chapter, I talk about how you can be supernaturally empowered to bless your child.

CHAPTER NINE

EMPOWERED BY FAITH

S o, you're ready to initiate the Honor Cycle by *Releasing Your Blessing*. But how do you muster up the ability to continuously bless your children, especially if your own parents have not showered you with blessing? It's no easy assignment! I find a lot of hope in the idea that *God empowers me to bless my children*. After all, He put me in this role. Certainly He's equipping me to do it well! I'm not alone. I'm empowered by faith. As a parent, you can take comfort in knowing that God is the source of love you need to raise your children, that He designed their unique identity, and that despite your occasional mess-ups, He will be faithful to finish His work in their lives.

God is the Source
Almost every wedding I've ever attended has included in the ceremony a reading of 1 Corinthians 13:4-8:

> *"Love is patient, love is kind. It does not envy, it does not boast, it is not proud. It does not dishonor others, it is not self-seeking,*

it is not easily angered, it keeps no record of wrongs. Love does not delight in evil but rejoices with the truth. It always protects, always trusts, always hopes, always perseveres. Love never fails."

I don't know about you, but this does not describe the kind of love that I find naturally flowing from me. First of all, my love fails. It actually runs out pretty quickly, even when I try to keep it up. It doesn't have that much patience, and it keeps score; it keeps track of every good thing it does for someone and expects repayment in some fashion. When I try to love people on my own, it doesn't come anywhere close to the description of love in 1 Corinthians 13! God's kind of love is different. In fact, many New Testament scholars assert that the unconditional love taught and exemplified by Jesus (termed *agape* in the Greek) is a concept that was previously unknown in all of history.[1] The ability to truly love your children and be a continuous source of blessing is not natural; it is an overflow from your relationship with God. It truly is a God kind of love.

This is good news! None of you have a parent you can look to as a model of perfect love. Left to yourself, you could only produce an imperfect natural love for your children, a love that's missing the overflow of blessing you need. But, in God, you have a model for perfect love and a continuous source of blessing to pull from. If you can access His love for you and experience His perfect blessing, you can plug into a source of unconditional love for your children.

---

[1] W.E. Vine, Merrill F. Unger, William White, Jr. *Vine's Complete Expository Dictionary of Old and New Testament Words* (Nashville, TN: Thomas Nelson Publishers, 1996), 382.

> ### GREAT! BUT HOW DO I ACCESS HIS LOVE AND EXPERIENCE HIS BLESSING?
>
> Good question. We were created to exist in relationship with God. However, that relationship was broken as soon as sin entered the world through Adam. Because sin separates us from God, we've lacked the full experience of His love and blessing. Jesus changed all that by becoming the path for man to get back into relationship with God. Just as one man's sin separated us all from God, one man's righteousness reconnects us. Establishing that relationship with God is the first step to experiencing His love and blessing on a daily basis. Check out "Empowerment to Live It" toward the end for more information.

God is the Designer

Here's another thought that brings me solace: God designed my children. God designed all the people around me. He may not have intended every choice they've made or every situation that they've had to face in this imperfect world, but deep inside each person, beneath the mess, is a perfect God-inspired creation.

> *"For You created my inmost being; You knit me together in my mother's womb. I praise You because I am fearfully and wonderfully made; Your works are wonderful, I know that full well. My frame was not hidden from You when I was made in the secret place, when I was woven together in the depths of the earth. Your eyes saw my unformed body; all the days ordained for me were written in Your book before one of them came to be."*
>
> Psalm 139:13-16

My faith in God as the designer of my children can actually empower me to bless them in moments where my natural mind cannot. I can see them (and other people) not only by their actions and outward appearance, but by the original design. I know that seed of His design sits on the inside of them. Everything that He's spoken about them in His Word is part of that design. Sometimes releasing a blessing is simply believing what He has said about them instead of what I see happening in front of me. God has said my daughter is the "righteousness of God in Christ Jesus" (Rom. 3:22). God has said that "goodness and loving kindness" will follow my son all the days of his life and that "he will dwell in the house of the Lord forever" (Psalm 23:6).

I'm not suggesting that you live outside the realm of reality. We live in a messed up world where people don't live up to their original design. Children are born with a human, sinful nature that tears at the God-given design on the inside of them. On top of that, they have hurtful experiences that reinforce wrong belief systems and an internal identity that counters that original design. Because of this, behaviors that don't support their God-given design must be confronted. But their identity as perfect creations of God can also be affirmed. Knowing that His Word upholds everything in creation, including your child, gives you the ability to bless him in any situation, to speak the truth of God's Word over and above any behavior that you see. (Heb. 1:3) God says His Word doesn't fail.

> *"So is My word that goes out from My mouth: it will not return to Me empty, but will accomplish what I desire and achieve the purpose for which I sent it."*
>
> Isaiah 55:11

The Bible also teaches that faith is "assurance about things that we do not see" (Heb. 11:1). When it comes to my child, the behavior I see is not the end of the story. I can use faith to see their potential, including the things I don't see yet in reality. As long as my wife and I agree with our children about the things that God has spoken over their lives, they will come to pass!

God is the Finisher

My confidence in my own parenting is also buoyed because the Bible describes God not only as the author and designer, but also as the finisher! (Heb. 12:2) I have a significant role to play as a parent, but I'm not the final say in what becomes of my children. The Bible says that "He who began a good work in you will carry it on to completion until the day of Christ Jesus" (Phil. 1:6). That knowledge doesn't drive me to apathy, but gives me hope for times when things will inevitably cycle out of my control. There is a God who created my children, and He has a purpose for their lives. When I can't do anything about choices they're making, or when I feel powerless to influence them in the right direction, God is not powerless. He will finish the good work He started in my children before they were even born.

You need never lose hope, and you can continue to agree with God's plan by speaking words of blessing over your child. I often think back to the path I was on early in high school. Faith was not a big part of my life. I valued independence over life-giving relationships. I believed in the power of my will over any other force. I was arrogant and hurtful, and I lacked moral clarity in many areas. I wasn't looking for God. I didn't even know how bad I needed Him in my life, but He found His way there. He didn't leave me on a path toward imminent destruction. When I thought I had it all figured out on my own, He inserted Himself and changed my life forever. He was faithful to watch over His design for my life. At the right moments, He has always adjusted my course to keep me on track. Think back to your most challenging outbursts of doubt, rebellion or pride. God didn't leave you in that place. The same God that was working in you then is working in your child now. Place your trust in Him. Partner with Him by affirming the seeds of greatness He has placed in your children. Let your words call that divine design on the inside of them to fruition.

Faith and Blessing in Operation

As I'm writing this, Frank (not his name) is locked behind bars. He faces a trial in a few weeks that may result in his incarceration for many, many years. That would be many years of prison on top of the last 20 years he spent making the poor choices that led him there. His behavior was dishonoring. His decisions were destroying his life. But his mom maintained hope in God's plan for her son and has started using the power of blessing to bring him back around. His mom wrote to me and said,

> *"When my son left our home at the age of 14, it was devastating. When I finally understood the importance of affirmation, I began doing this with my son. I continually spoke over him and to him God's Words of life and freedom and hope. Nothing is more important in one's life. It has taken over 20 years of loving him through one bad choice after another. But I now see so very clearly how God loves us through so many bad times and never leaves us or forsakes us. After years of loving him through poor decisions, our relationship has finally healed. He is honoring and loving me. He often says and writes from prison, 'I love you, Mom.'"*

In the moments where things were completely out of her control, Frank's mom turned to prayer and trusted in God's original design for her son.

> *"When we do not trust God for our lives and for our children's lives, we can become controlling, believing that we know best for our children's lives. But adult children need to know and trust*

God for themselves. We are not their Savior; Jesus is. During Frank's time of moving from jail to jail, all we could do was pray. From the last two letters that we have received from him, he's walking with God in a real relationship. Finally! Frank wrote that in each of those jails, God sent people to encourage and strengthen him."

Frank has a long way to go to walk in the fullness of God's original design for his life, but his mom can see the God-given potential in him and continues to call it forward. She is seeing huge results—not just from her own efforts, but from others that God is sending across Frank's path, wherever he finds himself. I know that the God who began a good work in Frank is faithful to complete it!

"Do not be anxious about anything, but in every situation, by prayer and petition, with thanksgiving, present your requests to God. And the peace of God, which transcends all understanding, will guard your hearts and your minds in Christ Jesus. "
Philippians 4:6-7

PART THREE: PRACTICAL APPLICATION

CHAPTER TEN

THE CYCLICAL EFFECT

I n 2004, Dr. Emerson Eggerichs published the book *Love &
Respect.[1]* In it, he asserts that a woman's greatest emotional
need from her spouse is love. For a man, it's respect. He also
describes the cyclical relationship between these two needs. A
woman who feels loved will usually automatically display respect
toward her husband. A man who feels respected by his wife will more
easily exude love for her. When the cycle is flowing, the relationship
blossoms and the couple grows closer together. When the cycle is
clogged, the relationship begins to deteriorate. My experience with
the Honor Cycle is that practicing honor and releasing blessing work
together in the same way.

Releasing a Blessing helps Children Honor

When I was in college, many guest speakers visited our church, some
of whom had a unique ability to hear what God was saying and
communicate it while praying over others. I was raised to be pretty

---

[1] Emerson Eggerichs, *Love and Respect: The Love She Most Desires, the Respect
He Desperately Needs* (Nashville: Thomas Nelson, 2004)

skeptical of such claims, so you can imagine that my posture was not immediately one of honor toward these people. Rather, I took an initially critical approach, watching from a distance, looking for holes in their theology or impure motives. Yet as soon as the speaker began praying over me, my posture quickly changed. It didn't take much, just a sentence or two about how God sees me, the significant person that He had created me to be, and my heart was turned. I thought, "This person hears from God! What an amazing gift!" I was prepared to believe and follow most anything else that would come out of their mouth. The blessing they spoke over me automatically resulted in my honoring them and their gift. Even as a child, the more someone would affirm me, the more weight I would give to what they had to say. This wasn't only because of my ego, but because I felt like they could identify the greatness I felt God had put inside of me.

Practicing Honor helps Parents Release Blessing

I've also seen the Honor Cycle work the other way, where a posture of honor invited a blessing. A few years ago I had the privilege to speak at a night service in my parent's church, the church I grew up in. While I was preparing my message, I felt an impression from God to use the opportunity to publicly acknowledge my dad as the great father, mentor and role model he's always been for me. I shared how his words of wisdom had paid huge returns in my life, and how his example as a servant leader in church had shaped the way my siblings and I are committed to our own church. For me, the result was a really powerful moment in our relationship. When the service was over my dad showered me with words of blessing, affirming me as a speaker, as a young father, and as his son. Because of our personalities, it's not easy for people in my family to affirm one another, but that moment was a special one for me. I really saw how honor can open the door for affirmation in a powerful way. As a result, our relationship grows stronger than ever.

Who Starts?

After you've identified a cyclical relationship like this, a natural question to ask is, "Who goes first?" Who should step out and jump start this cycle? I remember sitting in Dr. Emerson Eggerichs's marriage seminar, surrounded by couples looking for help improving their relationships, when this question came up in regard to *Love & Respect*. He paused for a moment, looked up at the eager crowd and answered, "I always say, let whoever is most mature go first." What a perfect response! It shifts our thoughts away from who owes whom and who has neglected whom the most, to who is ready to take a step toward healing or improving the relationship. Who is ready to put themselves aside for a moment and put the other person first?

Of course, with young children, parents have the first opportunity to speak blessing long before the child even understands the concept of honor. But an adult child is perfectly able to kick the cycle off by looking for ways to honor their parent. It really doesn't matter who starts. The trick is to be selfless, preferring the other, meeting their needs with no expectations in return. If you can accomplish this, you'll see a huge difference in your relationship that will grow for years to come. Over time the other person will likely begin to respond naturally in ways that meet your own needs.

Final Thoughts

I have a vision for my children that they will grow and accomplish much more than I'll be able to in my lifetime. I try to remind myself every week that any of my success simply elevates the platform that they start building from. Likewise, I believe that whatever my generation can accomplish in dealing with the issues of our day and improving the lives of people all around the world is only a stepping-stone for what future generations can do. That vision can become a reality only if we can pass along the lessons learned from one generation to another. My children will merely repeat my mistakes and at best retake the ground I've already taken if they're not positioned to build from the platform I'm building today. We need to strengthen the cycle of honor and blessing to build families and a society that endures and prospers through the ages. Building strong relationships between parents and children is important not only for the enrichment of our own lives but for generations still to come.

I challenge you to be bold and take a step toward releasing honor toward your parents and those who are like parents to you. Take deliberate time this week to bless your child or someone who looks to you as a parent. The next few pages close with practical ways to practice honor and blessing in your relationships. Once you start down this road you'll find new meaning and purpose for your life and your relationships. The Honor Cycle will take hold and the benefits will be seen for generations.

30 IDEAS TO PRACTICE HONOR

Remember that Honor is not an action. It's a posture of the heart. No amount of action can make up for a heart that is not honoring. However, the following actions are great ways to practice working honor into your lifestyle and releasing what's in your heart.

1) Show Interest.
   I know your life is way more interesting than your parents'. However, taking time to understand their passions will communicate enormous value.

2) Visit.
   For Real. When's the last time you initiated a trip home?

3) Be Responsive.
   It's hard for parents to feel the honor you have for them if they also feel like they're on the bottom of your to-do list. If your parents reach out, answer the phone. Return the email. Let them know they're important to you.

4) Communicate Appreciation.
   Dig deep into your chest of memories and find the right things your parents did that made you who you are. Then thank them for it!

5) Seek Advice.

    Honor values and puts weight on the input of parents. Before you make your decision, sincerely seek out what your parents have to say.

6) Forgive.

    No parent is perfect. Recognize they're just human (like you) and let the past slip into the past. Then the healing can begin.

7) Write notes.

    I started sending hand-written notes to my grandmother while she was suffering from dementia. They gave her a daily written reminder that someone loved her and appreciated her. It may be old-fashioned, but it still carries a lot of weight.

8) Hold the Door.

    It's a little gesture that says, "You are more important than me!" What else so clearly communicates a heart of honor?

9) Pay for Dinner.

    "No, Dad, I've got this one. You've done so much for me; let me at least do a little something to say 'thanks.'" Enough said.

10) Show up with Questions.

    I used to have an employee who came to every meeting with me armed with a list of questions. Every time it pulled the best out of me that I could offer. I felt like she respected me and wanted me to weigh in.

11) Show Public Gratitude.

Get the entire family together and some friends and their coworkers. Tell them all how great your parents are. Show the rest of the world that they're special. By the end of that day, they may actually believe it!

12) Call.

Pick-up the phone and check-in. It says a lot.

13) Bring the Grandchildren.

If you've got children, share them with their grandparents. Don't withhold their legacy from them.

14) Assume You Don't Know it All.

I'm wired to believe that I know best about everything. I have to be intentional to remember that I need input from my parents. I try to make sure I do a little "self-talk" before engaging my parents in conversation.

15) Provide Financially.

If your parents hit hard times and you can help, help them! No parent wants to be in this situation, but sometimes it happens. Send a check. Bring them in. Help them find counseling help if they need it.

16) Arrange Quality Time.

One time when I buzzed through town, I took my dad out to a movie. Turns out it was a remake of a movie he saw with his dad! I could tell it meant a lot to him. Many of our visits home are busy trying to do family time together. Find the quality one-on-one moments. Do a project together. Make a special visit.

17) Speak Respectfully.

It's funny. Sometimes we spend the least amount of time monitoring our language with the people we are closest to. Don't censor your feelings. Figure out how to communicate them respectfully.

18) Cherish their Legacy.

Parents need to know they have and are making a difference in the world around them. Think about how they've made an impact and remind them how special their contribution is.

19) Make It Easy On Them.

Parents carry a large sense of responsibility for their children. Purpose to make their job easy. Don't give them a hard time for trying to be good parents. Receive the blessings they give, even if it's not done perfectly.

20) Tell Them What You've Learned.

If your parents have taught you something that has helped you, let them know. It communicates value and adds to their legacy.

21) Seek First to Understand.

This adage from Stephen Covey's *The 7 Habits of Highly Effective People* applies to every relationship. Make it your job to understand where your parents are coming from before presenting your opinions.

22) Pray For Them.

My Pastor always says that if you can get someone praying for something, it puts a hook in their jaw, i.e., they'll cherish what they pray for. Pray for your parents and watch yourself grow closer to them.

23) Represent Them Well.

My dad once told me that the best way for me to honor him is to follow after God. Just living a Godly life is the most honoring thing I can do.

24) Believe the Best.

Your parents are going to go through things. People will question their integrity at times and at times, people may be right. You may be the one person who holds out for the inner-jewel you know they are. Stand by them and believe in them.

25) Look Past Shortcomings.

Parents will let you down. They will make mistakes and do stupid stuff. Let what you can slide by and focus on the good stuff.

26) Ask God to Speak Through Them.

Look for areas where you can involve parents in your decision-making. Ask God to give them wisdom and speak through them. That will give you a very honoring posture.

27) Submit.

Say 'yes' more than 'no.'

28) Follow Their Blog.

Your parents probably don't have a blog, but if they did, would you be a reader? Make yourself an ambassador of their ideals. Echo their voice to your sphere of influence.

29) Presence Them.

Not too long ago I attended a funeral on my mom's side of the family when she couldn't go. I realized my role as an extension of her was extremely valuable and I could tell it meant a lot to her. Look for opportunities to presence your parents to others. It's honoring to do your good works on behalf of someone else.

30) Live Your Life to the Fullest!
Someone paid a price for you to have the life you have. Make the most of it!

30 IDEAS TO RELEASE BLESSING

1) Prophesy.
   Sounds spiritual right? It's actually simple. Know what God says about your child and speak it out. Be God's affirming voice to your child.

2) Show up.
   I love it when my parents stay an extra day in town so they can be in church when I preach. Just showing up for the things that are important for your child communicates so much.

3) Be Generous.
   The blessing is all about empowering your child to prosper. Financial gifts are a clear signal that you are with them and supportive.

4) Entrust.
   Find an area of responsibility that you can completely release to them. It sends a strong message: "I trust you. You have great ideas. Go for it!"

5) Write Notes.
   Old-fashioned, but powerful. We get hand-written notes from some of our parents and grandparents. They mean a lot to us.

6) Correct.
   Correction may not seem like a blessing. Done correctly, though, it communicates a strong sense of love and belief in their future potential.

7) Believe the Best.
   Even when your child blows it, it's your job to see the hidden jewel on the inside. Hold on to the goodness you know is inside them and keep believing for it to shine.

8) Expect the Best.
   Guard your expectations. If you are expecting them to make good decisions, they'll learn to expect it of themselves.

9) Support their Interests.
   Your child is different than you. Affirm the parts of them that you don't understand. They shouldn't feel they have to be exactly like you to have your approval.

10) Release them to Learn.
    When I was 17, my dad let me lose $1,800 in a business he knew would fail. He gave his advice, but let me learn from my mistake. He trusted me to grow from the experience. I should have listened. Instead, I learned to listen.

11) Forgive.
    Children can be hurtful, especially when they are dishonoring. However, unforgiveness closes the door that

blessing flows through. Communicate your hurt, but don't hold it against them.

12) Say 'I'm proud of you.'
These are some of the most impactful words a child can hear.

13) Commend Publically.
Look for moments to celebrate your child in front of other people.

14) Pay Attention To Key Moments
There are certain times when a child is very vulnerable to your words (conception, birth, adolescence, birthdays, baptism, graduation, marriage, new births). Show up for those moments and unleash the power of your blessing.

15) Watch Your Words.
There may only be a small difference between the words, "Your behavior is unacceptable" and "You are unacceptable." But that small difference is the difference between a blessing and a curse.

16) Tell Them What You Tell Your Friends.
When I go home, I sometimes run into my parents' friends at various places about town. I hear from them about all the amazing things I'm doing with my life. They have heard about things from my parents that I didn't even know my parents knew about. Some of them I didn't even know about!

17) Throw a Party.
There is a Jewish tradition where a dad will throw his son on his shoulders at a party and shout out, "This is my beloved

son in whom I am well-pleased!" It may look like a party, but it's a blessing in disguise!

18) Say, "You're a Great Parent!"
Of course you have critiques about how your child is raising their children. But do they know that you believe in them as a parent? Let them know. They may not say it, but they're looking for you more than anyone to affirm their parenting.

19) Talk About the Time You Blew it.
You know the time I'm talking about. You got angry or frustrated and took it out on your child. It may have been a little thing, but it left a mark. It left your child scared, confused or uncertain of your love for them. They're adults, now. Talk it out and take the confusion away.

20) Say 'I Love You.'
This was not spoken in my family growing up as much as it was implied. We've grown past that now and we let each other know how we feel. Life is too short to go one day questioning. Be clear. Say "I Love You!"

21) Separate Identity from Behavior.
Your child is not his/her actions. Affirm their beautiful identity. Correct their behavior.

22) Pray.
Even if you don't have physical access to your child, you have spiritual access. I believe parents have special prayer rights over their children. God hears your prayers and will work to bring your blessing to your child.

23) Let Yourself Be Impressed.

It seems during adolescence that parents feel the need to flip a switch from constant affirmation to "ego-checking." Don't be your child's worst critic. Be impressed when they're impressive and let someone else pick it apart.

24) Handle Report Cards With Care.

Report cards don't end with school, and neither does your child's capacity to tie their identity to the marks they get in life. Commend them for good grades but make sure they know that your affirmation is not tied to their success.

25) Be the First One 'On Board.'

When your child is about to take off on a new venture, be the first one to jump on the plane with them. Why wait until they prove themselves to others first? Be the first one to believe in their potential!

26) Say, "You're beautiful!"

Everyone looks awkward at the beginning of adolescence. I noticed in high school that some girls grew out of it and became confident, beautiful young women. Others didn't. I'm convinced now that had a lot less to do with genetics and more to do with what was being said (and not being said) at home.

27) Let Them Dream.

I love this about my mom. She never brings a "reality-check" to my dreams. Life does plenty of that already. Your child may need a safe place in you to dream. Listen and learn about the greatness inside them.

28) Acknowledge Good Choices.

It's easy to point out poor choices. It takes more effort to see and acknowledge the things they're doing right. Encourage them! Especially their attempts to show honor. It's not easy in today's culture.

29) Think Legacy.

Your influence does not end with your life. Keep a multi-generational perspective for what you do with your life. That will keep you focused on the important things.

30) Lead.

Sometimes relationships just take sticking to it. You're the parent. They're the child. When the relationship is difficult, fight for it. They'll remember you did.

EMPOWERMENT TO LIVE IT

You may be reading parts of this book thinking to yourself, "There is no way I could ever do what he's talking about with any kind of consistency." I don't blame you. What I'm suggesting is not a natural kind of love toward others. It would be safe to say that we humans are incapable of consistently demonstrating the kind of love we need to keep the Honor Cycle moving. Fortunately, we don't have to conjure up this love on our own. The book of Romans says, "God's love has been poured out into our hearts through the Holy Spirit, who has been given to us" (Rom. 5:5). When we receive God into our hearts, it's a package deal. We don't just get Him. We get His ability to love other people. It's a fascinating idea. The love of God has been poured into our hearts!

I'm not saying that you won't have to work at it. Even with God on the inside, we must still make choices daily to allow Him to dominate our lives. Over time, though, we see more and more of His character and His love flowing through us. The first step, though, is to invite Him in. If you've never asked God into your life, let me give you that opportunity right now. Consider this: God is Love. (1 John 4:8) The Bible says, "God demonstrates His own love toward us, in that while we were yet sinners, Christ died for us" (Rom. 5:8). God believes in you so much that even before you came to Him, He sent Jesus to die on a cross to pay the penalty for all of your screw-ups and for mine. All this so that He could welcome us back into relationship with Him. The opportunity I'm providing right now is simply to respond to His love. If you're reading this and you find yourself believing that God loves you that much, that's faith stirring up on the inside of you. Put that faith to action and say this short prayer aloud. When you do, you'll start a whole new life filled with the hope and favor and LOVE of God:

Father God, thank you for sending Your Son, Jesus, into the world to die for me. Thank you for raising Him from the dead so that I could spend eternity with You. I ask You to come into my heart. I make Jesus my Lord and my Savior and I receive my new life in you.

If you prayed that prayer, I believe that you've just started a new life in God. Here are some great next steps to help His love flow through you.

1) **Find a great church**
God didn't intend us to experience this new life alone. Surround yourself with others who are also growing in love so that they can support what God is doing in you. The best place to do this is in church. Contact me if you need help finding a great church.

2) **Start reading the Bible**
For a great example of perfect love to follow, read about the life of Jesus in the book of Matthew (the first book in the New Testament of the Bible). Then, start reading other portions of the Bible. Ask for God to help you understand and apply what you're reading.

3) **Contact me**

If I can answer any questions or do anything for you, please don't hesitate to contact me. There is a contact form on this webpage where I can respond to you directly: www.harrisonwilder.com/about.

FAQS ABOUT RELATING
TO YOUR PARENTS

How can I have a better relationship with my parents?

Not everyone grows up with a 'Leave it to Beaver' experience at home. Our parents weren't perfect. We weren't perfect. Now we're adults, though, and we actually WANT to have a relationship with our parents. The secret to rebuilding that relationship is the practice of Honor. Honor is one of the deepest emotional needs parents have from their children. Not only will Honor be extremely fulfilling for your parents, it will enable them to more easily give you the affirmation you're looking for out of the relationship.

Read more in "Redefining Honor"
Page 30

I'm an adult now. Why should I listen to my parents?

Good question. Most of us were anxiously waiting to get out from under our parents' roof. We wanted to be free from their rules. Why go backwards and reach out to them for advice? Think about it this way. What if every generation learned every lesson for themselves? What if we never passed along successes or failures from one generation to the other? Society would never advance. It would reset itself every 70 years or so. It's the same for you and your family line. Your parents, no matter how successful, are a deep reservoir of experience and wisdom. You may not believe it, but they have a lot to offer.

Read more in "The Commandment with a Promise"

Page 12

My parents don't have a relationship with God. How can I honor them?
It's difficult when you and your parents don't share the same convictions. How can you value their input when you know they're speaking from a different value system? Yet, God didn't put any qualifications on the Fifth Commandment when He said, "Honor your father and mother." This may help, though. Honor doesn't always mean obedience.

Read more in "Does Honor Always Mean Obedience?"

Page 47

My parents are controlling. What should I do?
Sometimes parents seem so overbearing that you feel you hardly have room to breathe with them in the room, much less have a decent relationship. The intentional practice of honor can actually help in these situations!

Check out Debbie's story.

Page 47

I don't feel supported by my parents. How can I get them to understand me?
There are few things more difficult emotionally than feeling a lack of affirmation from parents. Secretly we all crave their approval and support of everything we do. The good news is that you can do something about it! Parents have their own emotional needs. When those needs are met, they naturally respond with the blessing of affirmation that you need.

Read more in "The Cyclical Effect"

Page 83

FAQS ABOUT RELATING
TO YOUR CHILDREN

How can I have a better relationship with my child?

As your child is growing older, he or she requires one primary thing from you: your blessing. Your blessing is a powerful force for good in their life and the foundation of a solid, lasting relationship. Not only will your learning to give a blessing be extremely fulfilling for your child, it will enable them to more easily give you the honor you need out of the relationship.

Read more in "Releasing a Blessing"
Page 59

I'm finally an empty nester! Why do I need to be so involved in my child's life?

I think there is a reason we go on living long after our children enter adulthood, and it's not just to enjoy a few years of retirement before we die! Whether they realize it or not, your children need your blessing. It remains a powerful force in their life for your entire existence, and beyond!

Read more in "The Power of a Simple Blessing"
Page 62

I'm hurt because my child is so unappreciative of me. What should I do?
There are few things more difficult emotionally than feeling a lack of honor from children. The good news is that you can do something about it! Even adult children have their own emotional needs. When those needs are met, they naturally respond with the honor that you need.

Read more in "The Cyclical Effect"

Page 83

I totally disapprove of the choices my child is making. How can I affirm that?
There is a difference between "who" your child is and "what" choices they are making. It's possible to actually affirm their identity and release a blessing even while correcting inappropriate behavior.

Read more in "What About Correcting Negative Behavior?"

Page 68

My own parents never affirmed me. How can I affirm my child?
You may feel inadequate to give your children the love and affirmation they need because of your own experience growing up. Fortunately, your parents are not the only model that you can pull from. The Bible consistently refers to God as "Our Father." He's the model of perfect parenting.

Read more in "Empowered by Faith"

Page 74

I'm tired of trying. My child is beyond hope. Can you help me?
I've met many parents right where you are. You're discouraged. You don't see any hope that your child can turn around. But God promises us that nothing is impossible with Him. The power of your consistent blessing combined with faith can do the impossible in your child.

Check out Frank's mom's story.

Page 79

106

ACKNOWLEDGMENTS

Dad and Mom. I couldn't have asked for better parents. You've built an incredible foundation that our entire family has anchored to. Thank you for loving, teaching and for believing in me. I still have so much to learn from you.

Eileen. You are a gift from God to me and I appreciate you beyond words. Thank you for your unwavering support of this project over so many years. I love you. What a woman!

Peter and Alison. I don't take for granted that I have the most supportive in-laws of anyone on the planet. Thank you for investing in me and trusting me with your daughter.

Pastors Dennis and Donna. I continue to learn so much under your leadership. Thank you for creating a safe place to be planted and for allowing me to flourish.

Emily Bradley. You've been editing my papers since college. You help me say it like I mean it and that is so valuable. Friends like you are hard to come by.

All of those who allowed me to learn from and use their stories. Thank you for sharing.

Erin Richer, Angela Sarafin, Tim Woods. Thank you for taking time to read and provide feedback in the early stages of this project. Your encouragement meant so much to me.

Dr. James Bailey. I was so thankful that you took the time to read through my manuscript. I was floored that you gave such meaningful feedback. That meant so much to me.

Richard Dyas and Brian Williams. You stood by me and showed great support for this project during some hard days. Thanks for believing in me.

My siblings. Caleb and Ashley. Hunter and Joy. You guys are a constant source of encouragement for me. I love you so much.

The Capital City Church family. It's an honor to serve God together with all of you. Eileen and I love each of you dearly.

Pastor Mark Batterson. Thank you for taking time to talk with me. Your encouragement had a great impact on me.

Andy Scheer. I so appreciate the time you took to help with my writing. You were so generous with your feedback. It took me by surprise. Thank you.

ABOUT THE AUTHOR

Moving to Washington, DC from his hometown in the heart of South Carolina at the age of 17, Harrison Wilder desired from an early age to be a voice of influence. His zeal for politics and business was quickly overshadowed by a passion for ministry. Over the last fifteen years Harrison has developed as a leader and communicator at Capital City Church (www.capcitychurch.com), where he now serves as the Executive Pastor.

Harrison has two young children with his beautiful wife, Eileen, who is also on the leadership team at Capital City Church. They enjoy living in the DC area, taking in all the excitement it has to offer and living life with others who are passionate about making a positive impact in the world. To learn more about Harrison Wilder visit:

www.harrisonwilder.com